# A Traveller's Tales

# A Traveller's Tales

## Memoirs

by Michael John Walker

*A Traveller's Tales: Memoirs* by Michael John Walker.



For permission to reprint or for further information, send inquiries to: Publisher, Pretzel City Press, PO Box 119, Leesport PA, 19533, USA; otherwise, email contact via info@ pretzelcitypress.com.

*Credits:* The stories within this volume are entirely original by the author, as remembrances.

*Charitable contributions*: A portion of sales benefit the author's chosen 501(c)(3) charity, Shofuso Japanese House and Garden, Japan American Society of Greater Philadelphia, Lansdowne and Horticultural Drives, West Fairmount Park, Philadelphia, PA USA. *www.japanphilly.org.*

ISBN 978-0-9997851-7-1 (paper)

Cover art "dog in a ute #1" by Australian artist Alastair Taylor, atpaintings.blogspot.com

Back cover - family photo of the Walker Boys (and one more boy)

Cover and interior book design by Berge Design, *bergedesign.com*

## Haiku

Old friends are so smart:
Close or far, they hear your voice
And know what to say.

———————

Sickness may strike all
But still it hits as a shock.
What was I thinking?

*—Michael John Walker, 2018*

*Michael, Geoffrey, Stephen (l-r)*

# Acknowledgments

I thank my brothers Geoffrey and Stephen for their support and friendship, especially over the past decade of my illness. Geoff spent as much time in Japan (and more) as I did, and Steve and I are twins and grew up together, in Australia and Hong Kong. I have much to be grateful for, to them and their families.

And I am very thankful to my great friend and editor, Marian Wolbers. She has helped and inspired me, both.

Michael Walker
*August 2020*

*Strasburg Railroad, Lancaster PA, 2016: Conductor, Michael Walker, Marian Wolbers*

# Foreword

## An Appreciation of Michael John Walker and His Writings

*by Marian Frances Wolbers*

The entries arrived sporadically. As the editor and friend (from Japanese university days) who was catching these anecdotes as they came in via email for a decade, I realized in retrospect that I was on a mystery trip around the world—the kind of luxury trip where one signs up for the ride and arrives at one surprising port after another, not in any sort of sequential, alphabetical, geographical, or chronological order.

"This Is Your Captain" kicked off these anecdotes, inspiring more writing to spill forth from Perth to Pennsylvania. That piece is a tribute to Michael's father, a Cathay Pacific pilot, and honors a father-son relationship. Much later in the memoir process, distinct areas in which to house all these texts emerged, encompassing remarkable episodes of diplomatic dinners and trips and jogging back to Michael's schoolboy days in Perth and Hong Kong.

Therein lies the organic beauty of this volume. Readers can open the book anywhere to find a story, a joke, or a remembrance that transports the mind and heart through the eyes of a keen thinker and observer of life and culture. You can read the chapters in any order, wherever you're drawn on any given day. The specifics included in Michael's descriptions breathe with an air of immediacy. As a reader, I never knew anyone named "Satan Wu," for example; however, the author's telling of that cross-cultural curiosity (with regard to name-giving) was thought-provoking and amusing. You'll find wordplay galore, as in "Two Milks," plus a boatload of witty fun and comedy in "The Human Carrot" and "Royal Ties."

Heads up, though! This book may spark instantaneous urges to travel—to Tokyo, Istanbul, Macau, the outback of Australia, and beyond. It will also inspire laughter and fresh thinking. Readers will find much self-deprecating humor to savor; tales of human folly and foibles; sibling and family adventures; tender moments and heartfelt scenes; and the unique effects of having been formally educated in Australia and Asia.

Finally, you'll experience an insider's attunement to diplomatic protocol and discover a lovable author who holds a well-honed, finely tuned regard for the formalities and informalities of culture, language, and human behaviors.

Michael Walker's tales remind us that, as fancy or high-minded as we think we are or hope to be when we present ourselves in relation to others, there are always comeuppances and—mercifully—plenty of revelations along the way to fill us with sentiment and humility in equal measure of sweet and wistful flavors.

Enjoy the journey of *A Traveller's Tales*!

# Contents



## Part 1
## FAMILY - GROWING UP



## Part 2
## JAPAN AND MORE

# Part 3
# AUSTRALIA

## Part 4
## DIPLOMACY



## Part 5
## LANGUAGE FUN

# Part 6
## WORLD TALES AND ENCOUNTERS

# Part 7
## MICHAEL'S MUSINGS

*Mother with sons Geoffrey, Stephen, Michael (l-r, Hong Kong ca. 1966)*

# Part 1
# FAMILY – GROWING UP


This Is Your Captain

Boarding School, Perth

Captain Courtney of the Cadet Corps

Cathay Pacific

Don't Waste the Sand

Hong Kong in the 1950s and 60s

I Never Sang for My Father

Kai Tak and Small Aircraft

Kowloon Junior School

Malaya, 1963

Near Misses

Satan Wu

Wing Commander Plenty

Yao Yat Chuen

# This Is Your Captain

In the 1970s, invited passengers could still visit the cockpits of airliners. (In those days no passenger would think about opening that door UNLESS invited.)

Being the son of an airline pilot, sometimes when flying around Asia I was able to sit in the cockpit for takeoffs or landings. Not looking to follow my father into the trade, on those occasions I think I displayed only a polite interest in what was going on. But one year, when flying from Hong Kong back to Tokyo to resume studies at a Japanese university, I happened to pay close attention while my father made the usual in-flight announcement after takeoff. Fortunately so.

"This is Captain Walker from the flight deck. Thank you for flying Cathay Pacific Airways. I would like to welcome you aboard Flight CXaa and advise you of our anticipated flying conditions. We expect to arrive in Tokyo on schedule at xxpm, and the weather is forecast to be fine with the temperature around bbC. While we anticipate smooth flying conditions, I recommend you keep your seatbelts fastened when not moving around the cabin." And so on and so forth.

Having switched the microphone off, he turned back to me and suggested cheerfully that as a smart-ass scholarship student I should be able to render the announcement into Japanese. I swallowed discreetly, took a few minutes to confirm the facts and to think of the words for altitude, speed, temperature, and humiliation. Then I made my first and only in-flight announcement, mostly in correct Japanese, and returned the mike with a sense of relief.

No sooner had I done so than the cockpit door flew open after the briefest of taps and a Japanese stewardess looked in. "Captain Walker," she said in obvious surprise, "I didn't know you could speak Japanese!" In memory, he looked around coolly and said, "Well my dear, there may be many things you don't know about me. I'm a modest person."

I give myself credit for not blurting out the truth. My father had a well-practiced sense of irony and he was a kind parent, after all.

*2016*

# Boarding School, Perth

In 1966 my twin brother and I started at a private boarding school in Perth. At first, we found it hard to understand the accents of the Australian boys, but we soon got used to it.

The other kids at the school were from country Western Australia and Singapore, Malaysia, or Hong Kong. Those kids were nice boys and mostly intelligent. On long weekends we went home with Australian boys to a farm in the countryside. We went to a dairy farm at Brunswick Junction, and I went by steam train to a home in Albany.

The school was good and some of the teachers very good. They were prouder of sporting than of academic achievement—but that was characteristic of the time. When my brother and I were in Year 11, we were selected in quiz teams on different TV channels. In my case, my team did well in our heat—until we were defeated by a team from a Catholic girls' school, who beat us on the religious questions. *Jesus Christ*, I thought.

Twice a year we were flown to Hong Kong to spend time with parents and friends. We were asked by Australian boys to buy and bring back for them some electronics. (Electrical things were cheaper in Hong Kong at the time.) Looking back, we were spoiled, but didn't think so then.

We continued to fly to HK while we were at school, and through to university.

*May 2021*

# Captain Courtney of the Cadet Corps

Alasdair Courtney was a teacher at the high school that my brothers and I attended in Australia. He taught several subjects, including Maths and Latin. As well, he was in charge of the school cadet corps, and he was a boarding master.

It may have been caused by this overexposure, but I thought Alasdair fairly absurd. He instructed us students to place our desks in rows, marked by him in chalk; and he wore military-style shorts that in summer made his "jock straps" visible. (Sexy it was not.) He resembled Captain Mainwaring of the English Home Guard, a series I saw at university (from *Dads Army*).

Undoubtedly, Captain Courtney's greatest moments were in the cadet corps. He was proud of his skill at teaching boys how to march, despite the lack of enthusiasm from them. There was something noble to his ability to ignore a student square-gaiting across the oval, while listening to a bag-piper practicing his unlovely instrument. The students marched about the school carrying unloaded World War One rifles, until one day we paraded off to the SAS base in the neighbourhood. The idea was that we were go-ing to shoot our guns at targets on the rifle range, but some (the farmers) were better than others (the city-dwellers) at this. Steve and I were among the other ranks, given our poor eyesight.

Steve's eyes were worse than mine, given that he wasn't wearing glass-es then. When it came time to fire the guns, Alasdair announced that Steve would be among the first shooters, and my feelings of interest in-creased. Bullets were fired from the prone position, with the cadets lying on the ground a little distance from the targets. Steve's first shots missed the target and ended somewhere unknown; "Cadet Walker," quoth Alas-dair, "you're supposed to aim at the target, not the sand." To give him credit, Steve responded ruefully but then laughed it off...

Some years later Alasdair Courtney retired from teaching and from military duties, with the proud rank of Major.

*April 2021*

# Cathay Pacific Airways

Cathay Pacific is a major international airline that was founded by two American and Australian pilots in 1946. It has always been based in Hong Kong and is controlled by the Swire Group of London.

Cathay now is one of the world's largest carriers of both passengers and air freight. Its flight crew has always been dominated by Britons and Australians. Both my father and uncle worked for Cathay for a number of years after the Second World War.

Both Dad and Uncle Peter had flown for the Australian air force in the latter stages of World War Two (in Papua and then-Portuguese Timor). My uncle left Cathay and Hong Kong in the 1960s to return to Australia; he worked for the Department of Civil Aviation in Melbourne, before becoming the first Managing Director of Air Nauru, a loss-leading regional airline. It flew to several Pacific islands—including Nauru—before terminating in southern Japan. It seems never to have made a profit...

With the expansion of the regional airline industry, Cathay Pacific grew rapidly from the 1970s. It re-equipped with modern planes like the Lockheed Tristar and Boeing 747. In its early days, Cathay suffered several accidents and incidents (no more than the industry average). But with the steady improvement in technology and equipment, the industry's safety record improved steadily.

Cathay's early record of occasional hijackings and shoot-downs was followed by a brief spate of accidents and violence.

*August 2021*

# "Don't Waste the Sand!"

In 1960 our parents took us on a long leave from Hong Kong to Australia—first to Sydney, then by car through the "bush" of eastern Australia and all the way to Perth on the west coast. (The long stretch of road from South Australia to Western Australia was unsealed then, although today it's high-speed bitumen all the way.)

To seven-and eight-year-old boys, this seemed a great adventure, but if memory serves, fratricide was avoided only narrowly on the road trip. Long games of "I Spy with My Little Eye" and the creative use of service-station passports saved the day, just. Traversing the Nullarbor Plain was especially boring: confirming the legend, there was not a tree to be seen. And other vehicles were scarce on the road...

Then somewhere west of Eucla, luck meant that we had to pull over—in a rather Saudi-like stretch of country. The fan belt had broken, with roadside assistance hours away. But not to worry: Dad put his mechanical skills to the test and converted the cord from an airline kitbag for the purpose.

Meanwhile, we boys played in the car's shade, building and demolishing piles of sand. To lasting parental mirth, I objected, saying: "Don't waste the sand!"

Immortal words, indeed.

*February 2019*

# Hong Kong in the 1950s and 60s

I lived in Hong Kong—first in Yau Yat Chuen, then in Kadoorie Avenue—from the age of four until twelve. My brothers and I attended Kowloon Junior School—a fine place—and briefly King George V High, before leaving for boarding school in Australia. (Afterwards, until our father's retirement from Cathay Pacific, we flew back to Hong Kong annually.)

We had classmates from Britain and Hong Kong (including a few of Russian and Indian descent) and some from Australia / New Zealand. As small, blond kids we became used to Chinese ruffling our hair "for good luck." We walked to and from school when older, past a nullah and we bought ice creams from a popsy-man. We watched noisy but cheerful Chinese funerals with fascination, and found family graves in the New Territories interesting, too. And I remember temporary stands built in summer near Sai Kung for colourful Cantonese-opera performances.

Of course, Death seemed remote—until a French classmate died in an air-crash in the Alps. A little later, the American war in Vietnam gave us the chance to inspect US aircraft carriers on HK Harbor. All in all, when as a family we visited London in the 1960s, it seemed almost like "going home." But later again, Cathay passengers and crew died tragically in a deliberate bomb explosion (over Vietnam).

From the age of ten, my life centered on a small yacht that our parents bought and moored at Hebe Haven. I remember swimming there after storms, and also the damage done to Victoria Harbor by major typhoons. And, in the days before cross-harbor tunnels, I recall taking the Star Ferry or a vehicular ferry to Hong Kong Island, to see a specialist or take a ferry to Lantau. Those journeys, and trips on double-decker buses, made Hong Kong seem more complete as a well-governed territory.

It was a big deal when the Ocean Terminal was completed in Kowloon in the 1960s. Together with the Peninsula Hotel (owned by the Kadoorie family), it was a bookend to shopping visits to Tsimshatsui. "No charge for looking," as the Indian storekeepers used to say...

*June 2022*

# "I Never Sang for My Father"

This was a fine movie, featuring Melvyn Douglas and a young Gene Hackman. I saw it many years ago.

Remembering the film now makes me think of Dad—and my failure to clarify some facts before he died in 2010. In any case, I believe the facts of his life are as I've set them out below.

Mervyn Walker was born in Fremantle in 1925, and he joined the Australian Air Force in 1943. He saw action late in World War Two, flying B-25 light bombers around Papua and New Guinea. Apparently, when a Japanese submarine was reported stranded on the surface, his aircraft was ordered to attack it, whereupon—no surprise—the submarine responded with fierce fire from its deck-mounted machine gun. Dad reported that the submarine was damaged but still afloat when his plane had to return to Port Moresby for fuel, and for a change of trousers for the crew.

After that war was over—and following a spell as a timber-cutter— Dad rejoined the Air Force to fly P-51Mustang Fighters. Just before the Korean War broke out in 1950, his squadron was posted for transfer to Japan, but—fortunately for us all—his own posting was canceled. For on the outbreak of war on the Korean Peninsula, 77 Squadron was committed to fight with United Nations Forces against North Korea and China, and lost several pilots shot down by MIGs in the process.

On leaving the Air Force again, Dad returned to Perth, this time with a young family. He was employed as an instructor with the local aero club, then worked for the regional airline, flying DC-3s from Perth up to Darwin. Then, from 1958 through 1987, he flew for Cathay Pacific Airways, based in Hong Kong, and operating gradually larger passenger aircraft (without glamourizing the story, a Japanese friend later called him "a Captain's Captain"). Quietly, we were all proud of him.

Merv's wife and our mother, Joan, sometimes worked in Hong Kong, as a nurse, a secretary—to the Chinese director of Kowloon Motor Bus— and as a relief teacher at a Chinese school. Their and our great pleasure was to sail, in the New Territories, a yacht they had bought when I was ten years old.

In those days cholera and other diseases were still prevalent in parts of Hong Kong, and I remember being woken by a tapeworm emerging from my intestine. A happier memory was of water shortages caused by sanctions from China—and, consequently—infrequent baths. Then from the mid-1960s, we boys began boarding school in Australia.

*September 2022*

# Kai Tak and Small Aircraft

The old airport at Kai Tak in Hong Kong—now redeveloped for other purposes—was known for its spectacular setting. Commercial pilots would say that flying into Kai Tak was like x hours of boredom, followed by 10 minutes of sheer terror.

After landing and clocking off, most Cathay Pacific pilots would repair to the Aero Club to drink—and critique "live" the landings of others—virtually next door.

The airport was used mainly by big four-engined planes: that's where the money was, of course. But sometimes it was used by light planes, too. Once in the 1960s, I had the (unpleasant) experience of sitting in the back seat while an instructor took my brothers for a spin in the skies nearby.

The instructor was a Flight Engineer—later First Officer and Captain, with Cathay Pacific. His jaunt took us over and around HK Island in updrafts—and back to Kai Tak. All the while, I felt increasingly uncomfortable, and regretful of the large breakfast I had consumed.

After Hal had touched down, it became clear to me that my breakfast would beat us to the Aero Club. Someone helped open the door as we taxied, and with relief I left my breakfast on the runway. Afterwards, it amused me to think of the next plane to land on that runway, perhaps skidding on my deposit.

*October 2021*

# Kowloon Junior School

In the early 1960s, I (we) were students at KJS (Kowloon Junior School) in Hong Kong. It was a nice school and had nice teachers. The language of instruction, of course, was English, with students coming from various countries—but all were competent in English.

There were around 15 children in our class. They were from 8 to 10 countries and territories that belonged to the British Commonwealth, the EU, and other countries. To list them in no particular order, they were: Hong Kong, UK, China, Australia, New Zealand, the EU, and the US.

From memory, the students in my Year 6 class were:
Michael (Australia)
Stephen (ditto)
Wayne (NZ)
Brian (NZ)
Ken (UK)
Brian (UK)
Brian (HK)
Jane (UK)
Elizabeth (UK)
Eustacia (HK)
Charles (Australia)
Jack (US), and others.

In addition, in other classes there were Geoffrey (Australia), Jan (Australia), Cathy Australia), Lynette (NZ), and many others.

Our (very good) class teacher in Year 6 was Mrs. Bramwell, from the UK.

*March 2021*

# Malaya, 1963

I was 9 years old in 1963, the year that we visited Malaya. The country (later the larger part of Malaysia) was newly independent and the mood was celebratory. Of course, that was several years ahead of the violence that occurred later between the Malay and Chinese communities.

We started in Kuala Lumpur and went on to Ipoh, George Town (Penang), and Butterworth. We flew by DC-3 in those ancient days and stayed in grand colonial hotels. KL was still gently paced, if very commercial, and the whole country seemed peaceful.

Ipoh is famous for its caves and was intriguing for young boys. Beyond that, I have no memories of the place. George Town, on the other hand, was vibrant and exciting. The colourful Chinese shops were exciting, although familiar from Hong Kong. The Indian snake-temple, of course, was doubly exciting, with its (slow) slithering serpents. Butterworth, where one of my father's ex-RAAF mates worked as a flying instructor, was a working airbase, and interesting for that.

From there we returned to Hong Kong, the family wanderlust satisfied for that year. (How fortunate we were...)

*April 2021*

# Near Misses

When I was ten or eleven, my parents bought a small yacht for weekend use, and as an excuse to get away from downtown Hong Kong. We boys thought it the greatest thing and took with enthusiasm to the boat chores assigned to us.

So I didn't complain when one summer evening my father asked me to stow the gear after an afternoon sail. I removed the battens, hosed down the deck and sails, and stuffed the sails into their bags. Then, pleased with my work, I stepped back off the deck of the boat, expecting to connect expertly with the close-by pontoon. Alas, I had misjudged the distance and fell backwards. I felt the back of my head kiss the pontoon, and then only the water closing over me.

For a big man, my dad could move quickly when he had to. Having heard the noise, he was onto the pontoon from below decks in one motion and pulled me from the water. Disaster averted!

Some ten years later on another summer night, in my father's pride-and-joy new Toyota, I drove my girlfriend back towards her parents' home in the Hong Kong countryside. Although I had both license and permission, she had neither, and foolishly I let her take the wheel part-way. Sadly, an unlit local driver decided to joy-ride that same night, and—sure enough—w,e collided. Fortunately, no one was injured, but the phone call to my parents was hard to do. Nevertheless, when Dad arrived by taxi at the police station and found the car to be drivable (by him!), he did no more than observe that driver-training was not for me to do.

When seen from a distance, all of us will have had some near misses in life. But actually, it's the few near-hits that worry me the more...

*May 2019*

# Satan Wu

As a child I lived in Hong Kong and had my early education at a British school there. In the 1950s and 60s, Hong Kong was a Crown Colony of Britain and there was little social mixing with the—always-friendly—Chinese population. The school I attended, for example, sadly admitted Chinese children only by exception—with most students being British, Australian or even local Russians or Indians.

My mother mostly was busy as a parent to me and my brothers, although for a period she worked as secretary for the Kowloon Motor Bus Company (managed by an Australian-born Chinese individual). But I remember more clearly the time when she filled in for a friend, who was away on leave, as a teacher of English at a local Chinese middle school. Many new schools were being built then to educate refugees flooding in from China, and, where possible, English was added to the Chinese-language curriculum.

This was of some interest to me, as an 11-year-old with no real idea of the difficulty of learning a strange foreign language. (After all, maybe I thought, that wasn't something Western children would have to worry about.) I remember finding the homework that my mother brought home for grading to be especially fascinating—when I was able to purloin some to read. I'm afraid the odd choice of words and the regular howlers would reduce me to hilarity.

I knew that many Chinese with the need or interest would adopt a Western given name, to be used in addition to their family and birth names (thus, for example, John Tse-tung Mao). For young students it was natural for their parents to suggest that name—from a book or a movie, for example.

This would produce many Philips, Janes, and Thomases. But one day, to my delight, I discovered in the grading pile that it had resulted in a student being listed as Satan Wu. I asked my mother (doubtless with a smirk) whether he was a good boy. When the answer came that sometimes he misbehaved, I fear I urged her then to say sternly, "Get thee behind me, Satan."

I don't think my mother made an issue out of my attempt at precociousness. And—in time—I became wise enough not to try for humour from people's efforts to settle within a new environment.

*2018*

# Wing Commander Plenty

When Dad had rejoined the Australian Air Force after World War Two, he was stationed for a time at Pearce airbase, north of Perth. He used to tell a story—apocryphal or no—about Herbert Plenty, the pompous commander of that base.

Apparently, Herb called a hangar one day, to demand to know about an overhaul happening to an aircraft. The telephone was answered by a typically laconic enlisted man. The conversation went like this:

"Plenty here."

"That's good. There's fuck-all here."

Unsurprisingly, the officer was apoplectic at this. He demanded to know who the man thought he was talking to, and was told he had no idea. "I am Wing Commander Plenty, commander of this base!!" Herbert declared.

The aircraftsman asked mildly whether he knew who *HE* was. "No, I don't" was the response.

The younger man said, "Thank Christ for that," and hung up.

*December 2021*

# Yau Yat Chuen

Yau Yat Chuen is a leafy suburb in Hong Kong. As a small child, I lived there for several years in the 1950s and 60s, before my family moved to an apartment a little distance away.

Yau Yat Chuen actually is—and means—"garden town." Most places there were two-story, with their own gardens. We lived in the bottom storey of a house owned by a HK Chinese family. As an older son was studying in Sydney, it made sense to rent part of their house to an Australian family.

One son taught my mother Cantonese ("Cheung sin sang yau yat ga che": Mr. Cheung has a car, if I remember). Many decades later, he and his family visited my parents in Perth. (Then he was a retired accountant, and he and his wife were looking after an adult daughter, struggling with a chronic illness.)

We lived in Dianthus Road. The house backed onto another rented by a Cathay Pacific family—with one more living on the other side of our street. Our amah and the Smith's communicated over the back fence—and one day, Ah Siu asked Ah Man whether she knew what had become of the Smith cat. It became clear that the "strays" van had been by that morning and had taken the moggie* away. Happily, it was rescued from the pound.

*October 2021*
**Moggie = A cat without a pedigree.*

*Water Taxi, Teshima*

Part 2
## JAPAN AND MORE

# Climbing Mt. Fuji

In the 1990s in Tokyo, my wife and I were friends with an Australian businessman and his wife. We had dinner together a couple of times and enjoyed each other's company.

Once we discussed climbing Mount Fuji, as foreigners did sometimes. John said that they had joined a climb of Fuji organized by the Japan-Australia Society. The participants travelled by bus to a kick-off point near the mountain and, after sleeping in sleeping bags, were to make an early start to the climb the next morning. A couple in the party were very friendly and noisy during the night, but no one said anything. Why would they?

At this point in the story, I asked ironically whether the couple had reached the summit the following day. One tried hard (sometimes too hard) to be droll...

Next day the participants assembled and began the climb. They all finished the day tired and sore—naturally.

*May 2021*

# Echo

In the 1990s, I was living in Japan with my wife and older son (the younger was at college in the US). Among our Tokyo neighbours were an older Japanese man "Komo" (an abbreviation of his surname*) and his French wife. Occasionally, we had dinner together and enjoyed their fairly eccentric company.

Komo ran a family jewelry business. He and Genevieve had met in Europe in the 1950s when he participated in a water-ski event in Capri. (How romantic, we thought.)

Usually Komo was close, even shy, about his early history. But while not giving much detail, he said once that, in the Pacific War, he had been drafted into the Japanese air force and had trained as a pilot. With distaste, he said he was involved in the (undefended) bombing of Shanghai by Japan. I didn't want to press on his feelings, but quietly filed the coincidence away (my father was in the Australian Air Force in the late stages of the same war).

At the end of the decade, Komo went to hospital for excision of a small cancer. Alas, things went tragically wrong. When we went to visit him, we found Genevieve distressed and agitated. The doctors had told her apologetically—never a good sign in Japan—that something had gone wrong with the anesthetic, and they were concerned about Komo's recovery.

It became clear that the hospital was (carefully) admitting a medical error, one from which Komo would not recover. He came out of the drug the next day, but not fully and only for some hours. We were allowed in to see him, and I remember his saying—in Japanese, where he had always spoken in English—"But the operation succeeded" ("*Sekkaku naota no ni*").

Soon afterwards, Komo fell into a coma. Genevieve insisted that he be kept in that state far longer than happens normally, and the hospital permitted that. When finally she consented to the withdrawal of life support, his body was laid out in their apartment for a couple of days (packed in dry ice, for by then it was summer). Following the funeral service, attended by us and many Japanese, Genevieve slowly rallied and oversaw the reading of his will and the distribution of financial assets.

A fascinating coda to Komo's life story came the following year. Genevieve returned from Paris, where she had settled as a widow. She had arranged for a wartime diary of Komo's to be translated and published, and I borrowed the text for a few hours. It told the remarkable tale of his survival of an air-battle in the South Pacific.

His aircraft had acted as pathfinder and escort for a flight of smaller planes, and, after its job was done, had turned alone for the long flight home. (None of the other airplanes returned from the mission.) But due to some kind of miscalculation, it ran out of fuel and had to make a planned ditching close to an island occupied by the Japanese military; I guessed it was in either the Caroline or Marshall Islands. As a result of skill or luck, or both, all the crew survived the ditching. A boat piloted by Japanese soldiers put out from the island and plucked them from the water.

However, once the aircrew had recovered from their narrow escape, they had to come to terms with a grimmer prospect. They found that the soldiers on the island were cut off from resupply (by the loss of naval superiority) and were beginning to starve. But after enduring many weeks of this situation, they were rescued by submarine—presumably for their value to a depleted military. They had to survive a dangerous and long return journey to Japan. But there they met a stroke of fortune, for the Japanese air force had become so stripped of aircraft that there was no assignment for them to take up. Thus the war apparently finished for Komo in dodging air raids, in his own turn.

Komo's life ended more than fifty years after a ruinous war and following a painful national reconstruction. There was great waste in all of that, but also much sacrifice and devotion.

*August 2020*
**Komorimiya was his surname.*

# Humour and Japan

Why don't we think of Japanese and humour in the same breath? Rules are hard to suggest on so serious a subject, but let me try.

### *Principle: The First*

Japanese are as addicted as others are to jokes—scatological or weird. If you're not convinced, look at TV in Japan: Think Monty Python on steroids. There is a whole category of dad-jokes, known as *oyaji* gags. Some of them are even funny.

### *Second Principle: Keep the Punters* Happy.*

In a Tokyo hotel, once I was approached by a young man with a program from a Vienna Philharmonic concert. It was clear that he wanted an autograph, so I found a photo of a violinist who resembled me and inscribed it from Henrik Schmidt. Fortunately, he didn't test my German.

### *Third Principle: Context Is All.*

I knew an Australian in Tokyo, a very good linguist, who told a story of wandering home one morning much the worse for wear. He was found by his Japanese wife as he was crashing into the furniture while attempting to disrobe quietly. When questioned, all he had to say was *"Chotto..."* for all to be understood, if not forgiven.

### *Fourth Principle: The Obvious Lie.*

I lived in central Tokyo, opposite a small house with a kennel and dog in the front yard. The dog barked a lot, and one night I went down to complain about the noise. After checking that it came from the other side of the fence, I rang the door and asked the owner to quieten his dog. "We have no dog," he said, unmoved by the fact that we could hear it as we were talking. I guess the joke was on me.

### *Fifth Principle: Modesty Is a Virtue.*

My first professor of Japanese at university (an American) was dry but sometimes profound. He said once to us, "Of course you have to study hard, but this is a difficult language, and I have a tip. If you're ever caught up in a Japanese conversation and find you've lost the thread, it's important not to panic. Continue studying your feet, but every few minutes look up and say '*Hehh*' or "*Haaa*.' You'll be taken to be a serious person." This was very sound advice.

*June 2019*
*Punter: a person who is betting on something*

# Interpreting & Being Interpreted in Japan

In Japan, not to rush in confers an advantage (unless you're a comedian!). It's good to be alert and to think before speaking. And cultural rules matter too—it's hard to undo a backslap or a smirk.

All this means it's sensible to think about how to use interpreting where it's provided. Fear not! But here are a few suggestions on how to act:

1. Hope for an experienced interpreter—but if it doesn't seem to go well, don't panic and worsen things.

2. Introduce yourself politely and avoid telling jokes (they WILL get lost).

3. Don't challenge the interpreter—missteps can be corrected later (like rendering "Japanese diet" as Parliament).

4. Speak in short, discrete thoughts and trust the interpreter. I heard one explain he was "translating ahead," and so he was!

5. Listen to responses and acknowledge respectfully.

6. Smile and thank the hosts—but not the interpreter (you can do that later).

*July 2019*

# Japan, Australia, and World War II

As the son of an airline pilot, when young I was able sometimes to use staff tickets for international flights. Once, when considering studying Japanese at university, I flew to Osaka with my brothers; we stayed with a Japanese family in Nara.

With our host, we visited her old high school nearby and spoke to students of English. Then we were ushered in to see the Principal; awkwardly, he had very little English—and we spoke no Japanese at the time. To give himself something to talk to, the Principal reached for an atlas. More awkwardly still, by pointing to the map of Australia, he indicated that he had nearly got to Darwin during the war.

After this encounter, we flew back to Hong Kong with our father. When my twin recounted the story, Dad said equably that we could have countered by pointing to Hiroshima on the map and saying "boom!" Undiplomatic, but a fair point.

Some years later I was in Broome, in Western Australia, with a Japanese businessman, and we happened to visit the waterfront during low tide. He asked innocently what the wreckage was that he could see protruding from the water. I responded truthfully that it was the remains of a Dutch flying boat shot up by Japanese aircraft, with great loss of life, after landing off Broome with Dutch families evacuated from Batavia. "Oh," he responded.

All of this backlit my father's late-war history. He mentioned once that, while on a reconnaissance flight over New Guinea, his aircraft flew over a Japanese submarine that was floating on the surface, apparently disabled. It bombed the submarine, which fired back with a deck-mounted machinegun. The crew made it back to base and proceeded to change their pants.

And, of course, Japan and its people suffered cruelly from the war.

*January 2022*

# Karuizawa

Karuizawa is a resort town in Nagano Prefecture, a couple of hours north-west of Tokyo. It is famously cool in summer and hence a popular place for golf and walking.

(When I was with the Australian Embassy in the 1980s, I drove there once with my family in the used Mazda we had acquired. I found the place alright, but then, in climbing the hill to the cottage, discovered how under-powered the car was. After dealing with a musty house and an irate wife, I elected to drive all the way back to Tokyo.)

Much later, when I was back in Tokyo with a different employer, I returned to Karuizawa by train with my sons and had a much better experience. We stayed at the old Mampei Hotel, with its high ceilings and alpine look, and found that it still had drawings in the public rooms that had been done by John Lennon in the 1960s (he spent several summers there). We enjoyed the hotel—it had been used by a couple of embassies during the bombings of WW2—and the avenues and stores were lovely.

Another summer, I stopped there for a coffee during a day-drive to Lake Nojiri (my family was travelling). It was a great drive, in a new car.

*February 2023*

# Kobe

Kobe, the main city in Hyogo Prefecture, is my favourite city in Japan. Parts of Tokyo have their champions of course, and Sapporo and other regional cities, too. But for me, Kobe has the right combination of climate and livability. As well, it is/was just hilly enough to offer good walks.

I visited Kobe regularly in the 1990s, as "Official Representative" of the Western Australian State Government.

Western Australia has been linked to Hyogo Prefecture, as a "sister state" since the 1960s (the original impetus came from the iron-ore supply link between the two regions). Kobe is a city of several million; it is less than three hours' travel from Tokyo by bullet train—close enough for husbands on solo assignment (*tanshin funin*) to return to their Tokyo families a couple of times a month.

Kobe has a thriving Chinatown, with the food and nightlife that go with it. And it has a popular commercial redevelopment of the old port district.

Kobe has history, too. Given its location, historically it was the centre of the trade in rice. But for me, in the 20th century it is associated with *The Makioka Sisters* (*Sasameyuki*), by Tanizaki. I remember the dramatic scene in that novel of the flood of 1940—tearing a young man from the upper floor of his house.

And I knew an ex-wool buyer—living in Ashiya—who had lived through that flood. A Japanese friend talked, long afterwards, of her father's emotion on farewelling American professors who were repatriated to the US in 1942, departing from Kobe Port by ship.

A favourite part of the city for visitors is the "protected" former houses of foreign residents. They provide a showcase for how foreigners lived in the late 19th century. (Nowadays, there are relatively few foreigners living in Kobe—with more in Tokyo and Osaka.)

In 1995, Kobe was crippled by the Great Hanshin Earthquake that killed more than 6,000 people. I remember seeing on TV the spreading fires in the city, following the earthquake. It was fortunate that the quake happened early in the morning: many of the cruelest deaths were caused by ruptures in the retail gas network and the resulting uncontrolled fires. (On the other hand, if it had occurred in office hours, there would have been an even larger loss of life in the city.) I remember seeing on TV the destruction that resulted. In fact, some of the most effective (and best appreciated) assistance that was provided to citizens afterwards came from the principal gang (*yakuza*) headquartered in Kobe.

From that point, Kobe turned its efforts to recovery in a way that Japan has made famous. The fallen flyovers, destroyed buildings, and ruined train lines were cleared away within months. A couple of years after the disaster, it was hard to remember that it had an earthquake had occurred...

*September & October 2021*

# Nagasaki

…Is one of my favourite places in Japan. It is well known as an area where Christianity emerged in the 1500s in Japan (inspired by Portuguese Jesuit missionaries). Some of them were crucified in particularly cruel ways— such as by having their crosses stuck into tidal waters east of Nagasaki, ahead of advancing tides. (*Silence* by Shusaku Endo has harrowing details.)

Nagasaki saw the development of a gun industry in Japan. It was a center of political dissent against the centralizing force of the Tokugawa Shogunate. And in the 1870s, there was a rebellion (the Seinan War) against the new Meiji government; it was led by a former colleague from Kyushu, Takamori Saigo. The outcome was the defeat, after less than a year's bloody fighting, of the Kagoshima forces and the death of Saigo. It was one of the last cases of the defeat of samurai forces principally armed with swords and spears.

Nagasaki is the setting, too, for Madame Butterfly, the opera by Puccini. In 1998, with my wife I visited Glover House (above Nagasaki's port). We saw the place where, supposedly, the married Lieutenant Pinkerton saw and fell in love with Butterfly. From there it all went badly, of course; that's why it is a tragedy, after all.

Nagasaki and its surrounding islands are one of the leading areas in Japan for tourism. They are justly famous for their beauty, and draw tourists from around the country and from other countries. There should be room for further development, if only Japan can hold a successful Olympics this summer.

The Japan Space Agency has most of its facilities in southern Kyushu. Its activities, and the unusual geological features on Tanegashima Island, mean that more attention is earned by the area.

*May 2021*

# Addendum to "Nagasaki"

For me and many, Nagasaki is a fascinating city. It is the centre of Christian belief in Japan—as well as the second city in the world to be attacked with nuclear weapons.

Portuguese missionaries, led by Francis Xavier, concentrated their efforts at proselytization on the southern Japanese island of Kyushu. They converted thousands in Nagasaki and surrounding areas in the 17th century; after Christianity was outlawed in the 18th century, many converts were cruelly put to death by the Shogunate. Those who survived continued to observe their religious rituals—but underground. As a result, their observation of Christianity gradually changed. When, after the opening of Japan in the1860s, those "hidden" Christians were discovered by the Vatican, they were not recognised for some years.

When I first visited Nagasaki in 1977, I had a different sort of encounter with a religious exile. I visited the historic cathedral (it had survived the nuclear blast through being sheltered by a hill), and met there an old Polish priest. We spoke for a short time, and I learned that he had resolved to live out his remaining years in Nagasaki, rather than try to return to a country that was ruled by a Communist dictatorship.

I visited Nagasaki again in 1984, with the Australian Ambassador. When we went to the Atomic Bomb Memorial, Sir Neil made (to me) a pertinent point. He observed that many more lives would have been lost—i.e., more than the number killed in Hiroshima and Nagasaki—had the Emperor not been driven to surrender to the Allies, by the scale of destruction in those cities.

Nagasaki is famous too as the site of the Puccini opera, Madame Butterfly, and for the movie starring Yves Montand and Shirley MacLaine (actually filmed mainly in Tokyo and around Mount Fuji). The opera is dramatic and beautiful musically, as you would expect.

The plot has a US naval lieutenant living in unwedded bliss with a young maid known as Butterfly. However, he returns to America and is reunited there with his wife. In the way approved in heroic tales, she forgives the husband after he confesses that he has left a paramour in Nagasaki, together with a small child. Lieut. Pinkerton duly reappears in Nagasaki— and briefly, joy is unconfined. However, overcome by shame and facing the loss of her child to Uncle Sam, Butterfly takes her own life (crashing minor key).

*October 2021*

# On the Road in Japan

During the university summer vacation of 1975, I decided to spend several weeks in central and northern Japan. I travelled mainly by train—at a time before bullet trains had arrived in those areas.

First, I went to Nagano Prefecture, having agreed with a fellow Australian student to work for a couple of weeks at a seasonal English school. I enjoyed the experience of teaching Japanese kids in the cooler air, playing traditional summer games with ("semi") crickets in the open. (It sounds naff, but really WAS fun.) Then I moved on a short distance to Ueda City, where the mother of a fellow Japanese student operated a *ryokan* (inn). I stayed cheaply for a few days, looking at the surrounding area.

Next I went to northern Honshu, where I had agreed to rendezvous with French and Japanese students from my Tokyo college—and travel on to Hokkaido. (The climate there was famously cool in summer.) On the way to Sapporo, we visited Noboribetsu, an old coal-mining town. We decided to go to a local *onsen*—a public bath fed by hot springs—there, at the urging of the male Japanese student who knew it. When we entered the bathing area, we discovered that it was a traditional "mixed-bathing establishment," and I (cheekily) discovered everyone would all be in the same naked boat... But to my regret, the place was steam-filled, and my glasses fogged up, so I didn't see a thing.

Then we moved on to Sapporo, where I met a Japanese professor and his wife whom I had met in Australia. Afterwards, I went on to to Wakkanai, at the northern tip of Hokkaido and on to Rebun and Rishiri islands, known as the closest spots to Russia.

*March 2021*

# Oshima and Niijima

Oshima and Niijima are islands not far from Tokyo (Oshima is the final radio checkpoint for Haneda Airport). They were popular in the postwar period as honeymoon destinations for Japanese, before international travel became possible for them.

In the "Golden Week" of holidays in 1975, together with my brother Geoff and other foreign students at Keio University, I travelled there by ferry. After an uncomfortable journey, we enjoyed our few days there. We stayed at a *minshuku* (private hostel) in Oshima, operated by a nice, middle-aged Japanese couple. We checked the old tourist traps, including the romantic horse-drawn carriages that aimed at honeymooners. And we "posed" for photos with each other.

Niijima no doubt was nice too, but my brief memory of it has disappeared in the mists of time.

*April 2021*

# Shizuoka

Shizuoka is an attractive part of Japan, close to Yokohama and the coast. It is famous for the quality of the tea, and mandarins, grown on its slopes. Of course, there is always the risk of an eruption of the nearby Mount Fuji, a dormant volcano. But the larger risk is of an earthquake—even "The Big One," triggered by the Pacific seismic plate.

From 2000 I visited Shizuoka a number of times, as the newest (and smallest) buyer of Australian LNG is based there. The President of Shizuoka Gas was a former trading company executive whom I had known in Tokyo. He was keen to introduce his staff to the international gas business, and of course North West Shelf was happy to assist.

I had visited Atami and Shizuoka City in 1976, with an Australian girl-friend. Then, in the 1990s, I went to various places in the prefecture with family and friends—even to a private aviary, owned by an artist. There are many places I didn't get to, of course.

*October 2021*

# Teshima, Inland Sea

Teshima is a small island between Shikoku and the Okayama coast of Honshu. There are legends around from the Sengoku period, as well as bridges and scars from the industrial present. It's still a pretty part of the Inland Sea. Teshima is known for its annual arts festival, but otherwise is quiet and bucolic.

In the 1990s, my family stayed there at a guest house owned by a large Japanese company. My wife and son and I were with Japanese friends and a family (mutual friends) from the Australian Embassy. After meeting at Matsuyama—for we had come from different directions—we took a ferry to Teshima to settle in for a midsummer break.

The excuse for the visit was a public holiday and long weekend, which matter in Japan. Takeo and Junko, our hosts, introduced us to the caretakers and showed us over to the bungalow, which was perched at the far end of the island—away from village and shops but overlooking the sea. The house itself was that odd sort of hybrid you see in Japan, with overstuffed lounges and tatami sleeping-rooms. There was a little platform off the beach, where the ferry dropped us so we could be winched in to shore. It was quiet and still after Tokyo.

Our friends Michael and Debbie were always good company, if distracted easily. After changing into *yukata*, we had a home-cooked dinner and pored over albums of house visits, before launching fireworks that had been laid in and then retiring to wash off the dust of travel. Next morning, we started on a fishing expedition, complete with rented boat and gear. Some baited and fished with more gusto than others, but as one we left the cleaning of the fish to our escort (the obliging couple who ran the place prepared our catch for dinner).

We returned to the island and its dock safely, only to find no one on the beach to haul us in (and keep our delicate toes dry). But fearing naught, I stripped down to my shorts, waded to shore and started the power-winch to drag my fellows in. Golf on the home green (we practiced putting on the private green, overlooking the sea and its passing commercial traffic) in the evening, and a feast of our catch completed the day.

After resting on our final morning, we lunched lightly over beers while waiting for the pre-ordered "water taxi." We roused ourselves when it arrived at the island, and all transferred on board after a reverse-winch. The way back, to Bullet Train Station and thus to Tokyo, was first invigorating and then monotonous. By degrees, it returned us to our urban lives.

*December 2019 & February 2023*

# White Man Reading Japanese Paper

After returning to live in Australia some years ago, I began a job in Perth with a Japanese company. I often commuted by taking a short bus ride to the river and then a ferry to the business district.

One summer evening I happened to tuck a Japanese newspaper under my arm for the ride home. I was still scanning it after the ferry, and so unfurled it on the pretty empty bus. Slowly I became aware that a man opposite was staring avidly at me. He was clearly Asian but not Japanese: he was wearing a longyi or sarong, and I could see his interest wasn't rude.

With five minutes left on my commute, I closed the paper and made eye contact. The man leaned forward courteously to talk to me, and this is what he had to say (in very correct English). "I've been living here for more than thirty years, but I've never seen a white man reading an Asian language before. Can you tell me what you have learned and how?"

I explained that I had learned slowly to read and speak Japanese during many years of study and work in Tokyo, and that I worked now for a Japanese company in Perth. He was a nice man, and seemed satisfied with my explanation. (Sadly, I never had the chance to visit Myanmar.)

*March 2019*

*The author in his garden, Fremantle*

# Part 3
# AUSTRALIA

# A Nice Bike Ride in the Desert (Not)

In 1997, there was a strange and alarming report in the Perth newspaper (I read it in Tokyo). A young Japanese man had been rescued in the middle of nowhere, on the Gunbarrel Highway, between Wiluna and Warburton in Western Australia.

By sheer good fortune he was found by a crew patrolling the unsealed road. Sensibly, the young guy was by a windmill, sitting in extreme heat with his feet in a trough that was refilling with water automatically. But—very oddly, given the trough—he was dehydrated and distressed.

After rehydrating the Japanese tourist (for such he was), the rescuers asked the obvious question: WHY had he not drunk from the trough? They received a memorable answer (but one that was understandable if you had been raised in Tokyo). It was that "the water was dirty."

This was a very fortunate end to a strange story. But such are the risks of solo adventure tourism...

*May 2021*

# Australian Bees

In Australia there are both native bees (that don't sting) and European honey bees (that do sting when alarmed). I knew that already, but was reminded recently by my Buddhist masseur, Bart, who has been treating me regularly at home for many years.

Earlier this year, at my request, Bart strung shadecloth from a gnarled old gum tree in my front yard. (The tree long predates my ownership of the place.) The shelter did the trick, of reducing heat and glare, and is popular with local wildlife—including Australian bees. The bees (and birds) are drawn by the flowering red gum, which produces prodigious volumes of flowers in summer.

This change has made me notice the bee activity more closely. This autumn, after gorging themselves on red-gum blossoms, bees have been falling in great numbers from the tree, stunned. Happily, many tumble into the shadecloth, where they sleep it off and then resume their bee lives. But many others fall onto the ground, where any ant cousins that become aware speed to this manna from heaven, which they envenom, dismantle, and consume.

This is nature at work, of course, as David Attenborough might say. But without disturbing the cycle, Bart picks up those stupefied animals that he sees and places them in the safety net. I've mentioned this to a few visitors, who add to the holocaust rescues as they leave. I find it all very interesting.

*April 2021*

# Australind

Australind is suburban and middle-class now. When I first knew it, in 1974, it was an even sleepier place.

Australind is a small town near the port of Bunbury, in Western Australia. In the 19th century, it was given that name from "Australia" and "India." (Already Fremantle was the main source of supply of horses to British India). From the 1960s, it became more prosperous, as the port and expanded when developed for timber and wheat exports.

In 1975, the summer before I travelled to Japan for study, I worked on a fruit farm near Australind—in order to strengthen my personal balance sheet. During the weeks that I worked, I drove one weekend to Australind with one of my workmates. He knew there was a "hippie" village out on the peninsula and so we drove out there. We were greeted by the somehow reassuring sight of wooden structures—until I learned later that the hippies were squatting on the land (paying neither rent nor for power).

In due course, the squatters were moved on to the benefit of property values.

*August 2021*

# Darwin

I visited Darwin only once, in 1986, as a member of a Chamber of Commerce "northern survey" tour.

The tour, by light aircraft, began in the south of Western Australia before going north and finishing in the Northern Territory. Once in the NT, we stopped in Katherine and saw its gorge and freshwater crocodiles. (One of my colleagues was related to the author of a famous account of the white settlement of the NT.)

Then we overflew Kakadu National Park before landing in Darwin. We all visited the casino there, where the "entertainment" was provided by a troupe of topless transvestites who pranced around the stage. The city had apparently become sophisticated.

*July 2021*

# Harold Clough

I got to know Harold after meeting him in Davos in 1990 (he was a member of a Western Australian delegation to the annual conference there, and I its manager). Harold was a fine man, always friendly and helpful.

Subsequently, I met him many times in Tokyo and Perth. He had studied engineering in WA and California, and had been friends with my mother when they were teenagers (later, I went to school with his sons). After taking on a family firm as a young man, Harold managed Perth's first major civil-engineering project, and oversaw Clough Engineering's move into the construction of iron-ore, salt, and gas projects in northwest Australia. Finally, Clough Corporation expanded into Southeast Asia, including the construction of oil exploration equipment.

Harold Clough died in Perth in 2022, at a very advanced age. He had lived a large life.

*March 2023*

# Kalumburu

Kalumburu is a small, isolated mission settlement in the tropical far north of Western Australia. It's the sort of place that nobody visits by accident, even in the dry season when the road is passable. It has a lot more than its fair share of social traumas, but with the support of the Church is doing its best to improve the lives of its few hundred Aboriginal residents.

On the day that the informal northern inspection tour dropped in for lunch, the resident priest was away on his aerial pastoral rounds. But after the three light aircraft had landed at the airstrip, several vehicles drove across from the settlement and acknowledged the arrivals, laconically but warmly enough. Unsurprisingly, they were driven by full-blood Aboriginal men, representatives of the self-governing community.

It happened that I was the only visitor to climb into the cabin of one of the four-wheel drives that had pulled over by the planes. I wasn't bearing any of the lunch-boxes that had come with us from the previous stop, so there were no bags to transfer into the "ute." (The boxes of beer that rather weighed down the planes remained within them, out of deference to the nuns awaiting our arrival in the Residence.) The driver, an older and rather grizzled man, observed me with interest but said little in response to my greeting.

As we covered the short distance to the mission buildings (bombed by Japan in WW2), I was conscious of Laurie—that was his name—continuing to look me over silently. I attempted polite conversation a couple of times, without success, despite sensing that he wanted to ask something; as a visitor, I didn't want to force the issue. But finally, as we approached the little settlement, I asked Laurie whether maybe he had a question for me. That pricked the silence.

"Don't you remember me from all that time in Derby, boss?" he asked in a hurt tone. In response to my comment that I had never been to Derby, that this was my first visit as far north as the Kimberley, Laurie remained silent. I repeated the fact, but in a moment of inspiration added that my twin brother had worked in that town (as a solicitor for the Aboriginal Legal Service). That did the trick.

As he pulled up and parked his vehicle, Laurie became quite animated. He told me of the pride he had felt in working for my brother and of the fair way in which he had been treated. (Understandably, he was less interested in hearing about the time I had spent in Japan.) He asked me to wait while he fetched his British Empire Medal, awarded for his quasi-legal work in Derby, and took a commemorative photo of me, the twin brother. What were the odds, after all?

Afterwards, Laurie—who was chairman of the community—joined the visitors when we were given a walking tour of Kalumburu by a somewhat broken-down Brother. After seeing the river and the crocodiles lazing on its banks, we walked past a yard where an old man was sitting out in the open, attended by flies and dogs. "Why isn't he living in one of the houses?" asked a German banker who was part of the tour. The answer pulled us up short. "Because he was a cannibal in his youth," replied the brother, "and after finding Jesus and repenting his behaviour, he swore never again to eat pork—a food consumed in the community." A whispered aside told us that the taste of pork was close to that of human flesh and was an unbearable reminder to the penitent of his sins.

Happily we had finished our lunch already. Following our walkaround and after thanking our hosts, with our pilots we returned to the chartered aircraft and resumed our flight, heading for Kununurra and Darwin. On the way back to the gravel runway, we passed a B 25 Mitchell bomber (a type flown by our father during the War) that had been left there following a crash landing in 1944.

*2016*
*aka "utility vehicle"*

# Kirribilli

During a visit to Sydney in the 1980s, I found myself with a spare afternoon. It being a nice day, I decided to take a ferry from Circular Quay (near the City) across the harbor.

After a fairly short ride—when I found myself thinking of Slessor's "Five Bells"—I disembarked at Kirribilli. Being aware vaguely that Admiralty House was close by, I walked from that stop uphill. Within a few minutes, I was in front of a large property with a sign that said I had found K House.

I couldn't enter the place without an appointment—maybe the Governor General was holding a meeting or the Prime Minister had borrowed the place. (Or maybe the ghost of Jim Cairns was chasing Junie Morosi around the pool.)

Like other places in central Sydney, like The Rocks and the Botanic Gardens, Kirribilli has a long history. It began life as a naval area (as the name of the Governor General's Residence implies), and the surrounding district was occupied by naval officers.

Properties in Kirribilli are owned by a small number of lucky people. But it is popular as a destination for tourists to visit.

*October 2021*

# Kookaburra

My parents-in-law had known a fellow-Italian couple in the southwest of Western Australia, who told this story from the 1950s.

The new wife had come out to Australia to join the husband, who had worked there for a few years, as a timber-cutter. She was from a town in Italy and was struggling to adapt to life in the Australian bush—especially as they had to live in a tent.

Things came to a head over the perforated-bucket bush shower they were using. His wife demanded that they buy a modest house in a nearby town—for her mental health (not that this term was used then). She was frightened and anxious over her belief that she was being spied upon by somebody while showering. Her husband assured her in vain that there was no one living nearby.

However, to placate his wife, the husband offered to stay back in their camp one morning. Sure enough, while she was showering after dawn, a distant but raucous laughter began. It was a kookaburra. This made a pretty good story—but didn't delay for long their purchase of a house, with human neighbours.

*December 2021*

# Lang Hancock

Lang Hancock—known to some as Long Hungcock—was a "station" (ranch) owner in the Pilbara region who helped develop the iron-ore industry in Western Australia. Following a long rise in ore prices, his company finally opened its first major mine in 2007, by which time Hancock Prospecting was controlled by his daughter, Gina—who had studied in the US and married an American. (The mine was developed jointly with an international major.)

In the late 1980s, I was involved briefly in Lang's earlier attempts to enter the mining industry. I joined a visit that Hancock had organized for a Czechoslovak delegation to Australia. We flew to Wittenoom, a now-defunct town built to service the asbestos industry, and landed at an iron-ore lease owned by Hancock.

That evening, we gathered at Lang's homestead above Wittenoom for a presentation by the man. A barbecue was cooked and served, and the group assembled outside for the presentation. Well, I thought, now we'll learn just how Hancock plans to finance his project, with its high extraction and shipping costs.

But no, we learned only how difficult evenings are for an old guy. When the lights went up from a home movie—so old that in it Gina was a teenager and Japanese I recognised were long-retired—Lang was fast asleep in his deckchair.

On my way back to Perth, I shared a flight with Ken Mccamey, another old-timer and self-taught geologist, who entertained me with tales of locating iron-ore deposits by following banded iron formations along ravines. So while no project was ever developed for the Czech market, my week wasn't entirely wasted.

*August 2023*

# Migrants to Australia

How good is Australia! (The Lucky Country…)

Successive waves of migration have benefited Australians a great deal—well, benefiting all except the Indigenous people. First came the English and Irish (many in chains) from the 18th Century. Next were the Italians and Greeks, from the early 20$^{th}$ Century.

After the Second World War, Greeks, Italians, Maltese, and various displaced people arrived in numbers. Chinese and Vietnamese followed in the 1960s and 70s, and then came the former-Yugoslavs. All have contributed greatly to this country, while working hard to improve their own families' welfare.

A former State Premier visited me this month. He told me an interesting story about relocation, and Australia and Japan. He had found that a former Australian Minister for External Affairs was descended from a missionary who lived in southern Japan. Her long life had ended in Perth.

As a professor of mine used to say, "Statistics tell the story, but a personal anecdote brings it home."

*October 2021*

# National Service

In 1972 I was in First Year university in Australia. I would have been required to "register" for national service (conscription) if the conservative government had not been defeated by the liberal Australian Labour Party. Fortunately, it was.

An incentive for first-time voters to support the ALP was created by Conservatives' crazy "Red Peril" policy. I made an unannounced decision that, if my birthdate was drawn from the barrel, I would refuse conscription as a so-called "conscientious objector." (How absurd was the process of selecting conscripts by lottery!)

When the conservatives—led by a particularly inept man—duly lost to the Labour Party in December 1972, a new government was formed by Gough Whitlam. His government introduced a swag of new and popular policies, including the recognition of China—and the ending of conscription.

Thank God for it.

*November 2021*

# Newman, WA

Newman is a small mining town in Western Australia, next to the large iron-ore mine of Mount Newman. It was built by BHP in the 1960s to supply high-quality ore to blast furnaces in eastern Australia.

I visited Newman from Japan several times during the 1990s. On one occasion, it was to accompany a delegation from the Japan Business Federation; the mission was led by Shoichiro Toyoda, who then was chairman of both the JBF and of Toyota Motor Corporation, the giant car manufacturer founded by his grandfather.

Dr. Toyoda was a quiet but engaging man, and after an inspection of the open-cut mine, we were invited to a barbecue put on by BHP. I was standing with Dr. Toyoda (to help with interpreting) when he said to one of the hosts that he had been impressed by the many Toyotas he had seen parked in Newman's driveways. He gave his business card to the man and asked him to contact him if any mechanical problems were encountered. "Naru hodo," I thought, "that gives new meaning to Toyota's slogan of continuous improvement."

This incident reminded me of something else that had occurred in Newman earlier that same decade. (While I didn't witness it, a trading-company friend of mine did.) A member of a similar steel-mill delegation attended a barbecue hosted by BHP's regional manager, a dour Scot who later was based in Tokyo. The Japanese man was affected both by the beer he consumed at the party, and by the comely wife of the manager. "Madam," he blurted out, "Your face is like a flower!" One of his colleagues—unable to resist—asked what kind of flower she resembled. "A cauliflower," he responded, no doubt to snorts of derision.

*January 2023*

# No Worries

When I was a student at the University of Western Australia, one of my Japanese instructors was a young man named Ippei Itoh. He spoke good English, as it was the language of instruction...

One day, Itoh-sensei asked me what Australians really meant when they said—as they did often—"No worries." I gave what I thought was a pretty good answer. I said, "They mean YOU might be worried, but I couldn't care less." (I was thinking of a situation where you'd just paid for something and someone had thanked you.)

While I was studying in Japan, Ippei disappeared to Italy to study opera. Some years after that, in Tokyo, I called an international property firm to ask about an advertisement for office space there. My call was answered by a now middle-aged Itoh-san.

We inspected a couple of vacant spaces together, before I thanked him, and said I would think it over. Finally, I elected to take space in an Australian Business Centre that was being established next to a major hotel. When I contacted Itoh-san to advise him, I remember his ironic response: "No worries."

*December 2021*

# Research in the Desert

Kalgoorlie is a big/small town in the large bare patch that spreads through central Australia; it was founded during the WA (Western Australia) gold rush of the 1890s. I visited it a hundred years on from that time, after being contacted by Japanese firms seeking assistance with their research on the regeneration of desert land. (They hoped to apply the results in Africa under Japan's aid program.)

When I visited Kalgoorlie (and its famous School of Mines), I thought more of west Texas than of Japan or Africa. But I found my introduction had landed well, and I gave it a small push along via the local radio station and a Welsh researcher with whom I palled up. On returning to Tokyo, I met again with the Desert Research group, joining a seminar convened at Tokyo University by its chairman, a Professor Matsumoto.

Despite a promising start and several research visits during 1996-8, the collaboration didn't flourish in the long run. There were various reasons for that, but I became aware gradually of one that complicated the work in a bizarre way.

In 1995 a series of bomb explosions occurred in Tokyo subway trains, killing a number of people and causing a sensation. These were the notorious sarin-gas attacks, carried out by members of a Japanese cult called Aum Shinrikyo—that, as it turned out, had already murdered several people. (My daughter normally commuted to work on one of those trains, but by great good fortune used a different line that day.)

It happens that the real name of the deranged leader of the cult was also Matsumoto, and he and some of his followers had visited WA to plan their crimes. They had leased a sheep station (ranch) well north of Kalgoorlie and, dressed in full protective gear, had tested their poisons on some wretched sheep. A local Aboriginal had reported their strange activity to the police, who tragically failed to follow up. The sheep "research" was reported in the local press, but only in a small way.

Predictably, perhaps, the police system subsequently moved into lumbering action. Professor Matsumoto told me (without rancor) that he was grilled on his next arrival at Perth Airport from Japan; I could do no more than express the appropriate sympathy. Histories sometimes intersect in strange and terrifying ways.

*October 2020*

# Rumania in Perth

In 1988, the late, unlamented dictator of Rumania, Nicolae Ceausescu, visited Perth. (He was overthrown and executed the following year, together with his wife.)

He was accompanied by Elena, his "scientist" wife, and their son and heir-in-waiting Nicu—notorious for his rape of the young Olympic gymnast, Nadia Comaneci. There was also a flotilla of thuggish security types: for my pains, as an official of the State Government, I was involved in some aspects of the visit.

My first contact with official Rumania was with a Consul from the Sydney Consulate-General, called Mr. Valcea. (He was responsible to the Ambassador in Tokyo.) Mr. V was more sophisticated than many official East Europeans of the day, and his practiced opening line was "My name is pronounced 'Vulture,' so why don't you get your jokes out of the way now."

I was asked to be part of a meeting with a large General in the "Securitate" (the Rumanian KGB), to explain unfamiliar customs—such as democracy. Aware of organized opposition in Australia to the Communist regime in Bucharest, the General demanded that protest leaders be arrested preemptively—in order to provide proper security for the distinguished visitors. He wasn't mollified by the response that that would conflict with democratic rights. Still—still, in the John Howard formulation—in the end, Australia got to determine who languished behind bars and who remained free.

Australia's domestic intelligence agency, ASIO, naturally was following the play. Its Perth director came to see me and asked my perspective on what was likely to happen during the visit. I told him that Valcea was on the hunt for "scenic" places to keep Ceausescu Junior entertained in Perth (and that he was pleading for financial assistance); I had said to Mr. V that Rottnest was one such place. I didn't hear how the reconnaissance went, but I was sure the young woman would have taken care of herself.

My final, modest contribution to the cause was to help put the kybosh on an attempt to extort an honorary degree for Elena from a Perth State university. I knew the PR person at Curtin University pretty well, and had a chat to him. I explained the concern in Canberra, and suggested he meet Valcea and listen to his request—but then fail to respond "because of bureaucracy" for the two weeks remaining before the "world-renowned scientist's" visit. It all worked a treat, and the honorary doctorate wasn't granted. What a shame...

Although I wasn't present, the final act in the drama happened as the visitors arrived at Perth Airport—in the gubernatorial Rolls Royce—for their return flight. As though spontaneously, a family of Rumanian exiles appeared from the bushes with a floral tribute for the visitors. The scene was captured on 1950s-style Rumanian movie-cameras, presumably to the gratification of the aristocracy in Bucharest.

*November 2021*

# South Western Australia

The South West of WA is an attractive part of the world. Its surf beaches and vineyards attract visitors from across the world. And the wildflowers, found a bit further north and east, are a magnet for visitors from Australia and overseas.

Margaret River and surrounding areas are by far the most famous magnets. But areas to the north are famous for spring wildflowers. (A shadow threatening the entire State is climate change.)

Climate change may affect rainfall and water levels, as well as the number of bushfires and even the sea level. The South West would become a less desirable place to live than it is now.

*August 2021*

# Studies in Dementia: A Citizen's Audit

This month, I am staying in a "respite room" in a dementia facility in Perth. It's a wing of a larger retirement home, about a hundred years old, near the Swan River in East Fremantle. (The respite is because of current renovations to my apartment unit.)

The place is comfortable, and the staff are patient; even the food is good. There's no coercion of residents, and no sign of Nurse Ratched. Given our aging population and the increasing incidence of Alzheimer's Disease, I think the results of my "citizen audit" are encouraging.

Of course, my visitors and I have the magic exit-code that other residents would like to have, too. That all means I'm free to observe the behaviours around me, at my leisure...

One of the residents went to the same school as me, albeit ten years earlier. He managed a real estate agency in Cottesloe, and when unsettled is happy to be asked to sweep the courtyard of leaves. He is, like most residents, nonverbal. A gentle West Indian points to the clouds and remarks on their evidence of God's benevolence (maybe he's right). Another, who is very verbal, likes to tell almost-plausible stories of how he built the home, and of encounters with guns.

The female residents fall into two types. Those in their nineties sleep most of the day, being wheeled out daily for bingo and airing. A younger woman is more or less "mens sana," but her personality is unusual: she bluffs people by shouting at those who ask her to be less loud.

*November 2021*

# Swan River

In recent years I explored various parts of the Swan River, lovely in season. Mainly, I went to the areas around Crawley and Nedlands, beautiful in summer and autumn. The river was always attractive, whether for a walk or lunch at a restaurant on a pier. And the University of Western Australia campus is always lovely.

In high school, with a teacher and classmates on a science expedition, we visited the river around Mosman Park in search of fossils in the bank. (In ancient times, the river was inundated before being exposed by a rise in the coastal plain.)

Upstream, the Swan winds into the plain—scattered with well-known and successful wineries like Houghton and Sandalford—popular and successful, too. They are fine for lunches and tastings in autumn and can be reached by a gentle ferry ride from Perth city.

The river is a lovely thing, both downstream and upstream.

*May 2021*

# Uluru

I visited Uluru in 2003, accompanying North West Shelf customers: it had been a bumper year and we were "celebrating success." We flew from Japan to Sydney, and then on to Uluru in a chartered Fokker 100. We stayed at the Uluru resort for a several days, before returning to Japan.

We went to see Uluru proper (the former Ayers Rock) early in the morning, and again in the evening for dinner. Before the main course, we were shown native delicacies by local indigenous people. To encourage the Japanese visitors, I sampled the cooked witchetty grubs; they were tasty, but no one followed my lead... After the entrée, we enjoyed a wagyu steak, and had an interesting presentation on indigenous myths of the origin of stars in the night sky. Altogether, a good time was had by all.

When I visited buyers after returning to Japan, the Vice Presidents of Chubu Electric Power and Chugoku Electric Power showed me, with pride, photographs of their Uluru visit. The latter didn't refer to his Akubra* being lost because of the high winds around the Rock.

*October 2021*
**A high-quality, Australian fur-felt hat*

# University

In the 1970s, I studied at the University of Western Australia in Perth (the only one accredited at the time). From 1976, I taught there for three years—before going to Canberra to work for the Australian Government.

UWA was (and is) a large and leafy campus. It has a big sandstone Arts Faculty and growing Science, Engineering, Law, and Economics & Commerce faculties. There was some—but limited—interaction between the Economics Department (where I belonged) and the Arts Faculty: for example, there were meetings between those who taught Chinese history and, likewise, Japanese Studies. (Whether they added to national welfare is a different issue.) And I saw some fine drama productions at the New Fortune and Octagon theatres.

But individuals left the greater impression on me. I got to know some gifted teachers of Economics (Ian Vanden Driessen) and Japanese (Ken Boston). And I met a well-known poet (Fay Zwicky), during a summer seminar on teaching methods. Sometimes I saw a famous playwright (Dorothy Hewett) stalking around campus. And a married couple (Ronald and Catherine Berndt), both pioneering anthropologists, were to be seen around campus.

Perhaps I should have stayed and developed my research skills. But that time is long ago now...

*November 2021*

# Wrong Way Ron

I worked for the Perth office of the major Japanese petroleum producer, Inpex, in the early 2000s (I had known it in Tokyo). At the time, it was preparing to develop a super-large gas and oil field that it had discovered off the north coast of Western Australia.

There were several Japanese, and two Americans, working in Perth for Inpex then. One was Ron, who had started life as a clearance diver in Asia, but then worked in the oil industry in Australia for many years. (The other was a reliable man who had worked previously for Woodside.) Ron was something of an industry legend: when employed by a local oil producer, he installed an offshore platform back to front. [He had (mis) directed a helicopter that was placing a "riser" on top of a well—despite protests from others that it was ass-backwards. Hence his nickname...]

I observed that Ron was able, and amusing too, but he had an unfortunate history of precipitating illness in those who opposed his views. A Japanese rival developed a usually-fatal tumor and was evacuated to Tokyo for medical treatment; he survived the illness but didn't return to work in Perth. Another man had gone through a painful divorce, but tragically didn't survive the stress of working for Ron. (A police report on his death made it clear that he hadn't braked before a high-speed collision with a tree, which took his life and those of his two children.) My own development of a long-term illness had nothing to do with Ron, but the strain of his deceit may have brought it forward.

Ron always had (declared) side-gigs happening, some of which made money and others not. He still has a substantial shareholding in an Australian firm that is  involved in oil exploration in India. I don't know how its staff are faring, but Ron was always a carrier of strain rather than a victim of it...

*February 2022*

*Foreign Service Intakes*

# Bruce Haigh

Bruce Haigh has died after a long illness. I knew him in Canberra many years ago, and afterwards ran into him around the country several times.

Bruce talked with some pride of his posting to South Africa in the 1970s, when that country was ruled by an apartheid regime. He developed relationships with Black opposition figures such as Steve Biko, later murdered by police. (He may or may not have informed his boss of those contacts, but the Australian Government of the day was happy enough to leave the question open.)

Bruce had several other overseas postings, around Asia, and later made appearances on TV as a political commentator. He lived a good life.

*April 2023*

# Good Intentions

By 1979, Australia finally had put behind it a long history of limiting non-pink immigration. The "White Australia" policy was no more, and liberals in this country breathed more easily. As well, the national cuisine began to improve from a low base...

In that year, the Secretary of the Department of Foreign Affairs hosted a reception in Canberra. It marked the end of a training program for entrants to his agency and for junior diplomats from Pacific, Asian, and African countries.

The Secretary of the day still was a fairly patrician figure, although he might have denied the description. Small in stature and short of sight, he made up for any accidents of inbreeding with great affability.

Upon entering the room, the Secretary dispensed with long words of welcome and began to circulate, drink in hand. One of the first people he approached was a dusky young man in conversation with an Australian. Sadly for the Secretary, he had chosen poorly for his opening sally.

The man with the dark skin, later to become Secretary himself, had been born in Africa to Indian parents but lived in Brisbane from an early age. Named Peter, he too was Australian, the beneficiary of a merit-based visa system.

"How have you been enjoying your time in Australia?" the Secretary asked, in deliberate and patient tones. "I hope you haven't found the accent difficult."

Peter was not one to be nonplussed, and he responded (in pretty broad Australian) that he was doing his best. "No worries on the accent," he said.

Having recovered himself, the Secretary resumed his journey around the room. The others continued on their careers, unperturbed by the significance of this exchange, if they had even heard it.

*April 2019*

# Koalas and Other Animals

Cute and unusual animals forever are part of Australia's interaction with other countries. But especially so with Japan! At the peak of the "kawaii" fauna boom in Japan in the 1980s, an Australian copper coin featuring the frill-neck lizard was so popular with Japanese tourists that extra supplies had to be minted to avoid stocks running low. But the true craze in Japan was for koalas—which, viewed up close, have the unfocused and appealing look seen in Japanese idol bands.

At that time, I was working for the Australian Embassy in Tokyo and sometimes fielded questions from the Japanese public on Australian wildlife. Several Japanese zoos acquired breeding pairs of koalas (shy little breeders), having spent large sums on climate-controlled enclosures and in arranging supplies of fresh eucalyptus leaves. This had the happy result in Japan of boosting both zoo attendances and the popularity of Australia.

One month the new Minister for the Arts and Territories visited Tokyo—"for familiarization." Together with the Australian Ambassador, he was invited to dinner by a Japanese developer, the invitation enhanced by adding the name of a major Japanese politician (reputed to be the money machine for the governing party). *Hmm.* Rounding out the party was a former member of the Australian parliament, a man with a taste for gaudy ties and gaudy friends, who happened to be in town on business. *Hmmm.* I was there on duty.

The dinner was at a discreet traditional restaurant behind Ginza. It featured quiet but classy furnishings, paper walls and tatami flooring that was fresh and pristine. A silent elevator took us up one level; then in our stocking feet we were delivered to our hosts in a private room.

Following introductions and drinks, two geisha appeared. They busied themselves, and the guests, with explanations about the food that was appearing dish by dish. Tongues were loosened by the alcohol and the mood was assisted by the geisha, with their clever conversation and ironic chat. But all the while the Japanese powerbroker sat silent and forbidding, speaking only when addressed. I recalled his media nickname: The Monster.

It emerged slowly that the developer planned to build a theme park at the base of Mount Fuji. He had options to acquire the land but lacked a wholesome symbol to pull in the crowds. What better than a family of koalas—to live in comfort in a corner of Japan that would be forever Australia? Perhaps the Minister could support supply of the animals, for the sake of friendship between the countries? The Australian businessman supported this idea warmly, although the Minister was silent. The Japanese politician blessed it monosyllabically. The Ambassador took all this in calmly but with a slow facial tightening. My own mind boggled quietly: two national symbols in one place—tied up by money and politics.

Any need for a prompt response was avoided by a pause for entertainment. The geisha moved to the end of the room, which silently rose a foot. They proceeded to give a display of Japanese dance, followed by a set of choreographed card tricks. Another combination of ancient and modern.

After more drinks were poured and appreciation was expressed, the evening approached its close. What kind of response would the hosts and their Australian businessman ally receive? I noticed the Minister and Ambassador visit the toilet together—an opportunity for consultation?

When they returned and after a polite interval, the Ambassador thanked the Japanese for their kind invitation and for a remarkable evening. However, he regretted to say that established policy in Australia prevented the export of native animals to any facility that had a commercial purpose. He happened to be aware of this from previous experiences overseas...

The Japanese must have been disappointed at this outcome, but naturally did not let it show. I never encountered again this settled Australian policy, but I was certain that both Mount Fuji and the world's koala population were the better for it.

*2016*

# Mr. Park's Contract

During the 1990s, I visited (South) Korea from Japan several times a year, to coordinate with the Korean man who represented Western Australia there. He was a former president of companies in the Hyundai business empire (he had fallen out with the autocratic founder and chairman, but I didn't press the matter).

Sometimes I called him "xx," from his initials, but mostly I referred to him as "Mr. Park" as other Koreans did. That seemed right, given his greater age, although it was hard to speak with any intimacy while using surnames. From Mr. Park and other contacts there, I had an impression of a country similar to Japan—but quite different too. The cliché of Koreans as the Irish of Asia seemed correct: drinkers, singers, and extroverts. Certainly, they were proud and sentimental. To a visitor, Seoul seemed a bit like the Wild East, making Japan feel as ordered as a garden. (Once, after being stuck in traffic on a bridge over the Han River, my car drew level with the cause—two Koreans having a furious fistfight over a small fender bender. Never in Tokyo...)

Mr. Park was financially independent and his family grown. He was fit and energetic and spoke excellent English, and Japanese too. We got along well, without becoming especially close.

The only time we really fell out was right at the end of our association. I was about to finish my assignment in Japan to take on an industry job, when I was asked to fix appointments in Japan and Korea for a senior State official (on his way to London to head that office). The context was that the Premier of the day was under pressure to cut spending—especially overseas.

Following polite meetings in Japan, it was clear to me that Bob was going to recommend closing the Seoul office. I felt philosophical about it, being more attached to the presence in Japan, but also aware of the need to surrender ground that couldn't be held.

The meeting between the three of us was at a restaurant in Seoul. Mr. Park had some sense of the issues, of course, intelligent as he was. I carefully left the talking to Bob, given my own imminent departure from government. The only reminder I made to Bob was of Mr. Park's name; they had met previously, anyway.

Famously, Korean family names are dominated by Kim, Lee and Park—the Smith, Jones, and Wilson of that country. The serious talk came after an initial toast from Bob, who seemed to have had a priming drink already. Unfortunately, from that point on, he referred to Mr. Park as "Mr. Kim"—and there was no stopping him (I tried!).

Mr. Park made attempts to negotiate a reduction to his budget, but he realized that the cause was lost. At the close of play, Bob and I made a point of thanking Mr. Park and agreeing to follow up and confirm in writing, but when we said goodbye—ostensibly still as friends—we had drawn a line under Mr. Park's contract. I didn't see him again, although I visited Korea once or twice on business and tried to call.

*December 2020*

# Royal Ties

The Heisei Emperor, who abdicated his throne this month, by all accounts was a fine Head of State for Japan and its people. Both he and the Empress will be remembered for a long time for their real compassion for survivors of the war and of natural disasters in Japan.

I met them a couple of times, once a bit before the Hanshin Earthquake of 1995—coincidentally in Hyogo Prefecture at a National Arbor Day event. I was accompanying a State Parliamentary delegation to participate in a tree-planting ceremony. In the evening, I lined up to attend a reception for foreign invitees, together with the State Parliamentary Speaker.

The Speaker ("call me Jim") was a bit overawed by the thought of meeting a foreign Head of State and his consort. As we waited, he confided that he had met the Queen once in London and had shaken that royal hand; he looked forward to repeating the honor in Japan. So he seemed crestfallen when a circulating official advised that, according to protocol, the Emperor did not shake hands and therefore guests kindly shouldn't extend theirs. Still, the queue finally delivered us to their Imperial Majesties, and we managed to exchange pleasantries and move on. I was struck by two things: the Empress' prodigious memory (she asked after a former Premier they had met on a visit to Perth years before) and by the fact that she extended HER hand to be shaken.

The next day we were reunited in Kobe with the others in the delegation, and I was curious to hear over coffee Jim's account of the reception. His memory of the event differed from mine in one respect: he told his colleagues that he had enjoyed the honor of shaking the hand of the Emperor of Japan.

I didn't have the heart to contradict Jim's version of events, but one of his colleagues with a robust Australian sense of humor added his own flourish to the account. He said, "Jim, I shake hands with an Emperor every morning." Jim fell into the (obvious) trap and asked what he meant, to be told that it was a Red Emperor.

*May 2019*

# Russian Embassy, Tokyo, 1997

After 1992, when the republics of the Soviet Union split off to go their own way, the large embassy that had housed them in Tokyo stayed in business. After all, Russia accounted for most of the staff—and of the profile in Japan.

And when the anniversary of the USSR's entry into the Pacific War rolled around each August, well-funded protests continued—near the modern-brutalist towers of the embassy. On one of those August days, I found my taxi locked in a traffic jam caused by protest vehicles, all blaring out wartime songs.

Rather than be late for a lunch appointment at the American Club that was close by, I paid off the driver and crossed the stalled line of cars to the pavement. First error. A belligerent and muscle-bound protester blocked my path, chested me, and abused me in crude Japanese. Still ignorant of my ignorance, I waited until a policeman waded in and pulled the man away.

By now rattled, about to clear the corner, I turned to look back at the aggressor. As he glared at me, I bent one elbow sharply under the other arm in a universal gesture. This was my second, and unforced, error. He broke free and roared towards me, looking like a medium-sized bull. As I stood preparing to be dismembered, the policeman effected a flying tackle—to his eternal credit.

Without pausing for further reflection, I turned and (briskly) resumed my walk to the American Club. In passing the nameplate next door, I was struck by a late and blindingly obvious thought—my close resemblance to the residents of the Russian Embassy, on this day all of them secure behind fortified doors.

*February 2018*

# Spooks

When I joined the Department of Foreign Affairs, twelve of us showed up in Canberra for induction. But a few days later a thirteenth appeared at table. We didn't need to be told that he was a member of the Spook species, sheltering in place.

As is the case in other missions, when I was transferred to the Embassy in Tokyo, there were several spies in the complement. Although most of their activities seemed misjudged (to put it mildly), a residual sense of obligation leads me to be a bit discreet in things I write here—decades later.

It was clear to observant local staff just who the spooks were. They would adopt a knowing look when asking about mail to be directed to someone "upstairs." (How would they, and non-Embassy Australians with social contacts, not suspect?)

I was friendly with the senior spook in Tokyo, and with his family. As to his deputy, I had known him slightly in a previous life, but always found him an unconvincing character (if jovial). We didn't maintain contact after his return to Canberra, but I learned that on a subsequent posting to the Middle East, he fell out badly with his Ambassador. Inevitably, he was recalled to Australia, but he wasn't done yet. He called in a friendship with a former Ambassador, and secured an appointment as a Trade official in South Asia. Resilience was part of the tradecraft package, I guess...

*October 2021*

# The Orse's Harse

The Defense Attache at the Tokyo Embassy, where I worked in the 1980s, had previously been posted to the High Commission in London. He had the annoying habit of referring regularly to his time at "The Court of Saint James." As a result, I thought of him as Big Ben, after the Japanese expletive.

One Friday I was on duty at the Embassy bar—a spell I often avoided—when I found myself in conversation with Big Ben and the Senior Admin Officer, a man I quite liked. The former launched on one of his anecdotes about London Society. He asserted that true English aristocrats always dropped the initial "h" that began words, while adding an "h" to the start of words that began with a vowel. He seemed to expect Des and me to be impressed by this information.

"Hmm," said I. "That sounds like an 'orse's harse to me." Des, at least, thought this a funny quip.

*July 2022*

# Train Traps in Japan

In the late 1990s I took a subway train a few stops back toward my office, after a meeting with a customer. I was carrying a generic bag with some (non-confidential) papers inside. On arriving at my stop, I stood to disembark, picked up "my" bag and stepped onto the platform.

Alas, in my complacency, I had failed to check whether there was an identical generic bag on the luggage rack. Fortunately for both of us, the young man whose bag it really was, was more alert and followed me on to the platform before the door closed. He took back his

bag apologetically and moved on to wait for the next train. Thanks to the efficiency of the subway system, I was able to retrieve my own bag later in the day—having learned a belated lesson.

Some ten years earlier, I had another unhappy brush with the traps of training in Japan. I had travelled with the then-State Premier and several attendants from Tokyo by Bullet train, everyone carrying small overnight bags.

We all climbed off the train at Osaka and proceeded a floor down, to line up for the taxis we needed for the next short journey. But I found that someone, no doubt with good intentions, had picked up a bag belonging to another. (After asking who it may have been, I realized from the silence that probably it was the Premier.) In the name of discretion, I personally proceeded to the Lost Property Office and handed it in, having explained what had occurred.

I'm not sure what the lesson was, apart from the need for care and for all to communicate well.

*May 2021*

*Travel fun in Japan ca. 1975*

# Part 5
# LANGUAGE FUN

# *Chotto Ne...*

Japanese is a hard language to translate, even compared to English. Subject and tense vary with context, and—of course—context matters a lot.

I knew a skilled interpreter / translator in the 1990s, in Tokyo. He worked with Japanese companies and Australian governments, and he wrote a regular column for a Japanese newspaper. He had a pretty subtle sense of humor.

Over a drink one day, Bruce recounted to several of us a story to illustrate how economical Japanese could be. (Typically, his delivery was dry and self-deprecating.) He said that after a long drinking session, he had blundered home early one morning, much the worse for wear. Inevitably, in letting himself in, he did a fair bit of crashing and banging.

After some time struggling to remove his trousers, Bruce added, he realized that his wife was in the room and observing him silently. He said that, thanks to the succinct nature of Japanese, he was able to avoid a long explanation and a heated argument. All he had to say, with appropriate gestures, was *"Chotto, ne..."* which, roughly translated is "A bit, you know..." And the rest was silence, if not acceptance.

Of course, what my friend didn't have to spell out was that his wife—like most Japanese—was smart enough not to waste time. There was plenty of time and space for the message to sink in naturally, with both parties.

*April 28, 2020*

# Famous Mistakes in Japanese

Once in Fukuoka I interpreted for a fine Ambassador, who was visiting the local power company. When Neil asked mildly—he spoke some Japanese—whether a phrase I had taken as "sukkari jikan" (ga nai) referred to a well-known Vice Minister of the Australian Department of Trade & Resources, I realised my mistake and corrected it. The reference really WAS to Scully Jikan...

I recovered from my embarrassment eventually, but I was glad I hadn't been landing with the Marines at Iwo Jima. Another mistake (this time not mine) was made by a well-known interpreter, who often worked for visiting Australian Prime Ministers. The Mitsui Chairman and Paul Keating were taking in the view of Kasumigaseki from the executive floor of the Mitsui Building. When the Chairman pointed out Japan's Parliament—known in Japan as "The Diet," Keating said he had always admired the Japanese diet. An understandable and amusing mistake...

*December 2021*

# Flesh Meat and Grog Land

When I was a student in Tokyo, after falling out with my host family, I shifted to a student dormitory. I walked past a butcher's shop every day, on my return from classes at college.

In the butcher's window was the legend: FLESH MEAT.

I say this not to poke fun at the owner, but because of the thoughts it provokes. As I—and maybe others—get older, I want to eat "meat" less and less. I enjoy sushi still, but can't bear the mouth-feel of flesh. (When at a restaurant I will order meat dishes to fall into line with others but would prefer not to.)

This issue is mine, and of course it's not the worst thing in the world. But certainly I've reduced my consumption of flesh.

Plus ça change, I guess.

This week I saw an amusing Facebook post from a former colleague, now living in Hokkaido in retirement. His name is Greg Lund. Greg had received one of those "We were unable to deliver" notices. It had the legend: GROG LAND.

*September 2021*

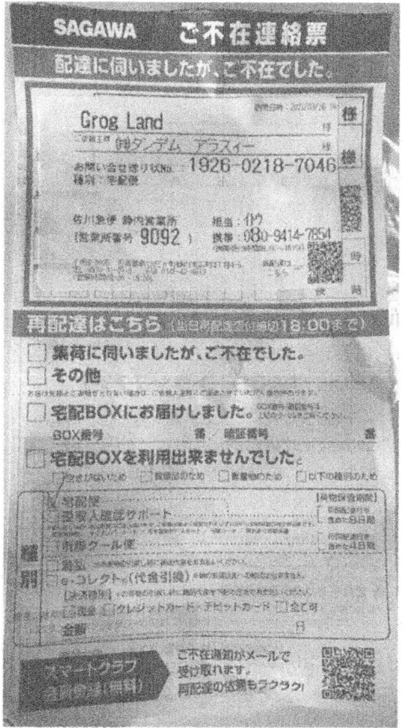

# Movies and Subtitles

Who doesn't like foreign films?

When I was a student in Japan, I saw several subtitled foreign movies and fell into the habit of reading the subtitles. While I wasn't quick enough always to catch them, I became addicted to the practice.

It was the Age of Peter Sellers, and I saw several of his films. His roles in *The Pink Panther* movies are justly famous, and in one he refers to Kato—his Japanese manservant who carries out surprise attacks on him—as a "yellow bastard." Surprisingly, the phrase was reproduced in the subtitles in full. (In the same movie, Inspector Clouseau, when asked "Does your derg bite?" replies that it doesn't. When the animal in question does bite the man, the unperturbable Clouseau observes, "Monsieur, that is not my derg.")

In perhaps the same movie, the phrase "olfactory sense" was translated, wrongly, as "sense of old factory." Nevertheless, I detected fewer errors in film subtitles than one sees in written advice in hotels.

*July 2022*

# Of Turkey and Japanese

In the mid-1990s, I visited Istanbul with my wife and son. We enjoyed it very much. We visited the Blue Mosque, the Aya Sophia cathedral, and the Topkapi Palace. All were attractive and deeply interesting for their historical value. And we liked the hotel where we stayed, a converted prison used for luxury accommodation, and within earshot of the call to prayer from a nearby mosque.

One day we went to a nearby center to see the tourist offerings. We were hailed by a shopkeeper who, not surprisingly, hoped we would grace his store with our presence. He called out, asking whether we were British or American. When I responded that we were Australian, he replied with tired cliches about Sydney and the Australian accent. Irritated by now, I responded in Japanese.

I was conscious that Turkish sellers of tourist stuff were adept at many European languages. But I was astonished to hear him reply in Japanese. (His Japanese was basic but correct.) Irritated by now, I said I didn't have much cash with me. To which he said insouciantly that he could change any currency into Turkish lire. I capitulated at that point and said I was tired and wouldn't buy anything that day; to that he said I was welcome to come back whenever it suited me.

*April 2021*

# Speaking Dickhead

In Tokyo, I was a member of a men's lunch group called—rather grandly—the Beefsteak & Burgundy Club. The origin story is that it was founded as an offshoot of a grander organization in Adelaide: that first club spawned others around Australia and then around the world. (I know the backstory, as I was secretary of the Tokyo club for a few years.)

The Tokyo club was notably informal in the way lunches were conducted—except that, at each event, members had to speak on food and wine. They did their best to be knowledgeable or witty on the subject, some more successfully than others.

Sometimes the speaker was a genuinely funny Irish lawyer. One Friday, Billy had the microphone and used it to bat away repeated interjections from a New Zealand colleague. His first riposte was "I've got the mic, not you; anyway I can't hear you." When the interruptions continued, Billy followed up with this classic put-down—addressed to members and restaurant staff: "I need an interpreter here! Does anyone speak Dickhead?"

I remember B&B Club lunched as a harmless keeping-in-touch activity. However, my successor was forced to resign over trumped-up accusations that—in one respect—were related to both the Beefsteak & Burgundy Club and to Speaking Dickhead.

*October 2021*

# The Human Carrot

Years ago, while living in Japan with my family, I heard an amusing and self-deprecating story from one of my kids' teachers at an international school there.

According to the anecdote, the teacher (an American woman) had a long train ride home every day after school. In that she wasn't alone, of course, but she also had to put up with sustained staring from men on the train. She was studying Japanese and decided to use her still-building language skills to challenge a man who was subjecting her to this silent pressure.

Unfortunately, in the woman's telling, she fell afoul of the difficulty of learning near-homonyms—as we all do. Meaning to say "*Watashi demo* **ningen** *desu yo*" ("I am a human, too"), she blurted out instead: "*Watashi demo* **ninjin** *desu yo*." Although she might have wanted to try a different phrase anyway, she had managed to declare herself a carrot...

As the teacher explained laughingly, this failed completely to rid her of the starer. Instead, he became even more fascinated by this creature.

*March 2016*

# The Jinguru Beru

Early summer, before the rainy season arrives, is a good time for train travel in Japan. The country is green and pretty and there aren't large groups of people on the move. One year at that time, I had the curious pleasure of escorting a senior Australian politician and his family on a visit to the world "cathedral" of a large new religion in the mountains of central Japan.* As experiences go, it proved to be charming and educational.

After a ride on the Bullet train, we changed to a local train at Nagoya and travelled at a more leisurely pace up into the Japan Alps. Having left the official program (and staff) behind, we were able to relax and enjoy the lush green and the rushing rivers that we skirted. By the time we arrived at a lovely historical town, it was mid-afternoon. I confirmed an appointment for the following morning with the church headquarters, and we proceeded to a small hotel where rooms had been booked for us.

It had become clear to me as we travelled that the interest in the religion (which was active in Australia too) lay with the accompanying family, more than with the politician himself. No matter: there was no reason to begrudge the use of a weekend for this purpose, following a busy official program. (But afterwards, I elected to keep the details to myself; there was no way of knowing where they might wash up.)

Following a good night's rest, it proved easy to find our way to the cathedral by taxi. The structure was something of a landmark in the town, with its Olympian proportions and rather Old Testament design. On arrival, an inquiry at the cavernous administrative centre produced a middle-aged woman who was to be our guide for the morning. As in all circumstances Japanese, the visitors' interest in the church and the religion was welcome, and an enthusiastic tour and briefing were provided.

I gathered that this was a syncretic religion, weaving together elements from at least Shinto and Christianity. It had been pretty successful in its short life, judging from the evidence of its head office. One of its central beliefs was in the healing power of the "True Light," when transmitted through one of its teachers. (But as open to enlightenment as I felt, I failed to see the Light when my turn came to be instructed. *Shikata ga nai*, I thought—it can't be helped.)

With the tour completed and questions answered, we thanked our guide and made our way back out of the cathedral. Then, as we waited for the taxi to reappear, one of our small party recognised an architectural feature. It was a free-standing bell tower from the European tradition, perhaps by way of Walt Disney. "Look!" she cried, "It's the Jinguru Beru."

*2016*
**Hidetakayama was the actual location*

# Two Milks

An old British friend who worked in that country's Tokyo embassy told me once of a funny experience he had there. I remember it because of what it says about the Japanese language, and the wisdom of both parties involved.

Eddie and his wife had moved back to Japan on posting, his second or third there. They lived away from the British Embassy, and in the normal way he took to shopping in local stores. At the closest one Eddie struck up a relationship with the elderly owner—based on the latter's curiosity about a foreigner speaking good Japanese.

His first purchase there was just a bottle of milk: *"Gyuunyuu ippon kudasai."* To this the shopkeeper had replied, courteously but with an unconscious international touch: *"Miruku hitotsu de ii desu ne"*—using the more Western noun (i.e., *miruku* instead of *gyuunyuu*). Making a mental note, on the next occasion, Eddie used that same term: *"Miruku hitotsu kudasai."* But the owner's response innocently inverted his formula: *"Gyuunyu ippon de ii desu ne."*

So, when he dropped in again, in order to avoid doubt, Eddie asked for two milks: *"Konkai wa, gyuunyuu ippon mo miruku hitotsu mo kudasai."* To this, the owner responded in good grace: *"Okyakusan wa oshare ga ojouzu desu ne"*—acknowledging his customer's wit.

*August 2019*

# Xabunguru

When my son was four, we returned to Australia from Japan, where he had been born. Naturally, he was influenced by his earliest years there—including from the wildly creative kids' TV programs in Japan. One of his favourite cartoons had been *Xabunguru*, about a transformer robot that conquered all before it. (What young boy wouldn't have loved it?)

He was a lovely child, and like most kids he loved pets. One day, a stray kitten found its way to our house, and Christian just had to keep it. When we asked what he wanted to name it, he said "Xabunguru." The reason wasn't obvious, but then he was five; of course, we acquiesced.

One day we attended a parent conference at his primary school in Perth. His Year 1 teacher said nice things about him. The only real question she had was why his cat had a strange-sounding name. We explained that we had just returned from Japan, where Chris had watched local cartoons a lot. The teacher was happy to accept our explanation.

*March 2021*

*On the Strasburg Railroad, Lancaster, Pennsylvania*

# Part 6
# WORLD TALES AND ENCOUNTERS


Bosnia in Asia

British Embassy, Tokyo

*Guten Tag*, Nippon

Herbie Wong, M.D.

International Centre, Keio University

Italy

Kosovo, I Never Knew You

London

Macau

New York City and Pennsylvania, 2016

O Turkey

Perth, Zurich, and Tokyo

Singapore

Sri Lanka

Switzerland

Taiwan

# Bosnia in Asia

Nearly twenty years ago I first met, on a visit to Perth, a Bosnian man with whom I later became very familiar. Besko had been Yugoslavia's trade representative to Malaysia when the civil war in Yugoslavia began. He was summoned by the Ambassador, his boss, and told that his citizenship had been revoked and that, as a result, he had no job and no home—except in Sarajevo, where he and his wife owned an apartment.

Such a situation was replete with ironies, of course. One was that he had few contacts outside Yugoslavia that he could use to find new employment. Fortunately, he saw a newspaper promotion of Western Australia, and contacted its department of agriculture, in which he had a professional background. He was offered an advertised position based in Vladivostok, for which he was well suited—in part because he spoke Russian from childhood.

Thus it was that I met Besko next in Vladivostok, where I had flown from Niigata, Japan. Together we had meetings with the Primorsky Krai Government and a South Korean trading company in Vladivostok. We also had dinner at an Australian-owned restaurant named after Captain Cook(!), that was owned by a Russian-Australian (allegedly with Australian intelligence connections: shades of John le Carré and all that).

On that note, I stayed in a new hotel that had problems with its plumbing (its taps emitted only rusty water). Only a day after my return to Japan, two men died in a bombing of their car in the hotel carpark.

Primorsky Krai was a lawless part of Russia, even compared to Moscow and Leningrad. When I went to visit a bank in Vladivostok with Besko, we were accosted just outside by a Russian, who offered a more favorable $US-Ruble exchange rate. (I preferred the bank's exchange.) A pistol was visibly poking out of the man's jeans...

As we were driven, in daylight, to Vladivostok's unsightly airport for my departure, another (slight) surprise occurred. In the middle of the rustic highway, there was an obviously drunk local who had passed out on the road.

Little wonder that Russian life expectancy was falling steadily...

*April 2021*

# British Embassy, Tokyo

During the 1990s, my wife and I were friends with the British Ambassadorial couple, whose near-neighbours we were.

Sir David had been ambassador to Korea before being promoted to Tokyo. Before that, he was private secretary to the Prince of Wales. (After returning to London, he established Britrade, modeled on the Australian original.)

The British Embassy dates from the late 19th Century, when the Japanese government granted land overlooking the Imperial Palace to the leading powers of the day. In many ways it was a self-contained community, with lines of two-story houses in the dignified style of that period.

The embassy had a couple of language teachers in Kamakura, and—as other embassies did—holiday houses in central Japan. In Tokyo, there was an outside pool within the compound: life as it was meant to be lived.

And Sir D tooled around in an MG...

*August 2021*

# *Guten Tag,* Nippon

I arrived in Tokyo early in 1975, in order to study Japanese at Keio University. Together with my brother, for the first few weeks I stayed with a doctor and his obliging family—they were related to one of our Japanese instructors in Australia.

During that time, I visited Shinjuku one weekend with Kenji and Kazuko (the doctor and his wife). We stopped at the Keio Plaza Hotel (no relation to the University) for a coffee, with me still fairly unsure of the order of things. After we had found seats and ordered, I became aware of being watched by a young Japanese man, who—as it seemed—was plucking up the courage to come and talk to us.

When he did, he made a beeline for me. He was clasping a brochure to his chest, that he presented to me with a pen—as though seeking an autograph. The brochure was a program for a concert by the Vienna Philharmonic Orchestra, held the previous night. Helpfully, he pointed to a photo (of a violinist, I recall) with a fair resemblance to me. Believing in giving the punter what he asks for, and quietly egged on by Kenji, I signed with a small flourish for Klaus Schmidt—it may have been.

The incident improved my social confidence in Japan no end, and I like to think of the memento lying for years afterwards in a private music-room.

*June 2020*

# Herbie Wong, M.D.

Herbie Wong must have been one of the first Chinese Australians to qualify as a medical doctor. That was in the 1950s, some time before Australia opened its borders to Asia. (The small number of Australians then of Chinese heritage were descended from the few Chinese allowed entry in the 1890s.)

Unusually for a non-Chinese speaker, Herbie moved to Hong Kong in the 1960s, in order to practice there as a doctor. He met there my father, who was working for the local airline. One day, Dad said, he was with Herbie at the Kowloon Bowling Green Club—which functioned mainly as an international drinking establishment. They were in the bar with another patron, who was most interested in this apparently Chinese man.

Herbie was asked by the man—evidently British—about his medical specialization. He bridled at this question from a man with the cultured accent and superior manner. "My specialty?" Herbie asked, and answered with the immortal phrase: "Pox, son, pox."

Herbie's succinct response had its no-doubt intended effect, and allowed all parties to resume serious drinking.

*February 2021*

*Note: In Australia, "pox" is a synonym for syphilis or any other disfiguring disease. (Yes, Australians have/had a sometimes cruel sense of humour...mjw)*

# International Centre, Keio University

In 1975-76 when I was there, many foreign students were studying at Keio's International Centre. They were from the US, France, Australia, and South East Asia. Many later became college professors and diplomats.

During that year we went on several school trips, to the Izu islands (self-organized), Lake Nojiri, and hot springs resorts in central Japan. (We also went to Waseda/Keio baseball matches and to sumo tournaments in Tokyo). All together, a "balanced program"—at least, that was the excuse in my mind.

There were friendships with Japanese students at Keio, too. I was an "audit student" in the Economics Department, which had excellent teachers. (But with still-limited Japanese, I struggled to keep up in class.) With Japanese students at Keio, there were self-selecting friendships; in the summer vacation when I was at Keio, I stayed at a *ryokan* (inn) in Nagano, operated by a friend's mother.

And we made lasting friendships among our "colleagues." In some cases, those friendships lasted a lifetime. But for me, the International Centre's attempts to find suitable host families left room for improvement...

*August 2021*

# Italy

I visited Rome in 1968, together with my parents and brothers. We didn't have time to see much more than the Colosseum, the Forum, and the more recent palaces, but I had a sense of the Italian style and chaos that fascinates the modern world.

Unfortunately, that was my only visit. In the 1990s, I proposed to my wife (who had aunts and uncles in Florence and La Spezia) that we visit Italy from Tokyo after our daughter's wedding in London. She rejected it, on the grounds that we would have to take suitable gifts for all her relatives. Rather, she said that we should choose another time to go.

Again, after my illness and retirement in Perth in the 2000s, I thought we should go to the Old Country. That idea, too, was re-declined, because "someone would have to carry other's cases." (I was still walking then, but with the use of an elbow-crutch.) And that was the last such chance.

*July 2021*

# Kosovo, I Never Knew You

In 2008 I was preparing to leave Tokyo and return to Australia, following a marketing assignment in Japan with Shell and North West Shelf. It wasn't clear that there would be an interesting job for me in Perth, and I saw an advertisement in the Economist for an Energy Advisor to the Government of Kosovo. By previous experience too, I was qualified for the position.

My then-wife was a dual citizen of Italy and Australia, and the idea of living in Europe appealed to us both. Notionally, I would work in Pristina, and she could live in northern Italy—

where I would contrive to travel from time to time.

This seemed like a good scheme, but it fell at the bureaucratic barrier of the United Nations. (At the time Kosovo was administered by the UN, following an attempt by Serbia to expel the dominant Albanian population and a subsequent intervention by NATO.)

I wrote to the nominated contact in Pristina, then tried to call him a couple of times. Finally, I had to give the idea away, and resume packaging for Perth.

*May 2023*

# London

I have been to London four or five times over the years, beginning when I was 15 and visited with my family.

Subsequently, I went there on business, on my way to or from Switzerland. I visited London on a few occasions over the years on business, especially following travel to Switzerland to attend a conference. Once, in 1997, I visited for my daughter's wedding. (She had been living there, and her swain was English, from the Home Counties.) The ceremony was done at a well-known church in Knightsbridge, a fashion and diplomatic center in London.

But my first visit, with my parents and brothers, was in 1968. We saw the tourist landmarks—St. Paul's, the Tower, and Big Ben—in the words of a pop song popular in the day. We stayed at a small hotel in Aldwych, on The Strand, and saw Buckingham Palace and Hyde Park, too. We visited the Imperial War Museum too, at our Dad's behest (Australian friends had served with the English Air Force during the War). I remember seeing a Lancaster and a Spitfire there.

When I visited in 1989, I went to Harrods for shopping and to Parliament to see Question Time in the House of Commons. The Mother of Parliaments, indeed...

*July 2021*

# Macau

Nowadays Macau—like its bigger neighbour Hong Kong— is becoming just another city in southern China. Not only has it been absorbed (inevitably) by China, but it had been dominated by it, politically and commercially, since the 1980s.

But in the 1960s and '70s, it still had a degree of autonomy. East Timor was yet a colony of Portugal, and Hong Kong's shipping news reported the regular sailings to Dili of a supply ship. And the weight of local tourism and of Macau's casinos—driven by the Chinese gambling addiction—mattered to the regional economy. Even in recent years, North Korean spies were drawn to fish in Macau's waters.

In the 1970s I visited Macau several times with brothers and family friends. In those days we travelled via the old, slow ferries from Hong Kong; the faster hydrofoils came later. We saw the highlights of that Sino-Portuguese city, including the ruins of the grand cathedral that was almost consumed by fire centuries ago. We saw the original Lisboa casino—I remember seeing amahs surrounded by piles of gambling chips, and we admired the gracious Portuguese houses.

I learned later the history of the place and its founding in the 16th century—well ahead of the larger and more prosperous Hong Kong. St Francis Xavier used it as the base of his successful Christian proselytizing in China and Japan, again in the 16th century. Macau became the early center of trade between Europe, China, Japan and India—as well as Brazil and Africa. (I remember seeing in the Hong Kong newspaper, in the 1960s, the sailing schedule of the small ship that used to sail to Dili.)

By the late 19th century, Macau had been eclipsed by the rise of Japan and the decline of Portugal. But it prospered still as the center of the gambling industry in Asia. By the 1980s, its prosperity depended on the monopoly granted by Macau (Portugal) to casino investors.

Around the time of Macau's reversion to China, the Macau Government (and Portugal's too) found the funds to connect the islands of Taipa and Coloane to the rest of Macau. It was a good investment, one that paid off quickly at a time of rapid growth.

In 1989 I met for lunch, in Perth, with the legendary Sino-Portuguese "businessman" Stanley Ho. (He resembled a James Bond villain,

I thought.) He was a "partner" of the Packer family and an investor in Western Australia, and for that reason asked to see a WA Minister. Who would refuse?

*July & October 2021*

# New York City and Pennsylvania, 2016

I visited the US, with my friend Gary, in summer 2016. We spent a couple of days in New York City and then went on to Pennsylvania by road. For me it was the first time to visit those venerable places, and it was thoroughly enjoyable.

We travelled on to Pennsylvania by hire car (driven by a pleasant driver). We gave a ride to a nice woman who was headed back to the same small city in PA.

We passed through Philadelphia and went on to Reading, where an old friend of mine from college days in Japan lived. (Gary and I stayed at a pleasant small hotel there.) Marian drove us to the college where she taught and to other places in Reading, and to the Amish country nearby. Reading is an attractive place and altogether we had a great time there.

After Pennsylvania, Gary and I left the US via New Jersey. I returned to Perth via Brisbane, happy and none the worse for wear.

*April 2021*

# O Turkey

My only visit to Turkey was in 1999, when I flew with my wife from Tokyo to Istanbul. (She had been there the previous year with our teenage son.)

We stayed in a hotel in the historic center of the city—a converted women's gaol. It overlooked a mosque, and in the mornings we woke to the lovely sound of the call to prayer. It (almost) was a cheap hotel by international standards, given the favorable exchange rate of the Turkish lire—then and now.

We stuck largely to Istanbul, going only beyond it by ferry, into the Bosphorus and on to the entrance of the Black Sea. We went past ancient sites on both sides of the Bosphorus—reminding me of *The Towers of Trebizond*, a delightful and true pre-WWII story of travel within Turkey and neighbouring countries, all by camel.

We went as well to the famous Topkapi Palace, dating from the 16th Century and the Ottoman régime. We saw too the ancient Hagia Sophia Cathedral, from when Istanbul was the New Rome. The nearby Blue Mosque was lovely and remarkable; the objects were so much check-by-jowl that I found fragments of ancient coins hard by the Topkapi Palace. History itself was threaded into the place.

We spent an interesting day lost in the Grand Bazaar, too. Turkey never felt unsafe.

One morning we came upon an underground cistern—not well advertised—that dated back two thousand years, to Roman times.

The food in Turkey was great, of course. There was ravioli in clear soup, for example. But the one that stood out for me was Imam Bayildi ("the priest fainted"), a dish of eggplants and other vegetables.

*August 2021*

# Perth, Zurich, and Tokyo

Perth is not a leading global city (nor am I a global figure!). Nevertheless, for a while in the 1990s, it seemed almost as if it were—at least in terms of corruption.

In 1990, the then-State Premier, Peter Dowding, led a business delegation to the annual meeting of the World Economic Forum, held south of Zurich. When I met him at Zurich Airport—I was manager of the delegation—he asked my opinion of a man nominated to become the next State Representative in Japan (I had accompanied Peter to Japan the previous year). I had to say I didn't know who that was: apparently, he'd been suggested by a friend in Tokyo. Finally, that man declined the offer made to him, and the job was offered to me.

After a successful WEF meeting in Davos, it became known that Peter Dowding had been toppled as leader of the State Labour Government— by a well-known fixer (Brian Burke) who had preceded him as Premier. To his credit, Peter returned to Perth and accepted his fate in a dignified way; subsequently, he moved to Sydney, where he opened a legal practice.

Burke had prevailed upon the Australian Government to appoint him Australia's Ambassador to Ireland & the Holy See, and it seemed a nice touch when—later—he resigned and was jailed following an investigation into his travel expenses. Several years after his release from prison, Burke was jailed again, this time for bribing a State public servant to rezone key agricultural land—to his profit and that of others. He was joined in that conspiracy by another retired politician, one who had attended the Davos meeting.

Of course, he isn't the only politician to struggle with relevance-deprivation syndrome after retirement. But his was the most egregious example of which I'm aware. It seemed like an episode of *The Sopranos*, albeit without the violence: Burke was driven by both talent and insatiable greed.

Following Burke's toppling of Dowding, a very able woman became Premier. She responded to the previous trail of corruption by reducing the class of international travel permitted for State public servants. Needless to say, this didn't touch the underlying issue...

*April 2022*

# Singapore

I first visited Singapore, by ship, when I was four years old (in 1957). From there we flew to Hong Kong, where Dad began a job with its airline, flying through the region.

From high school, we boys began to fly between Hong Kong, Singapore, and Perth annually, for family reunions. Singapore and the other cities were fairly quiet places then. But I remember visiting Bugis Street—a famous transvestite place—with an airline crew. (All part of the teen education, I guess.)

Whenever we stayed overnight (often with Dad), after a swim in the pool of the Singapura hotel, we would have an unofficial satay-eating contest (our record was 140, I remember). Once we visited the colonial-era Tanglin Club, with a British military officer, for a swim in its pool.

On another occasion we had to stay an extra night on the way to Perth, and were given a tour—by the hotel general manager—of the city, the causeway to Malaya and its plantations.

*July 2021*

# Sri Lanka

I "almost" was posted to the Australian High Commission in Colombo in 1984. At least, I applied for a cross-posting from Tokyo, on the grounds of hardship and maltreatment by a Tokyo supervisor. That was rejected out of hand by the Canberra bureaucracy, of course.

I had been interested in the former British colony of Sri Lanka since the 1960s, with its remarkable mixture of races and cultures and its peculiar history. I was fascinated by this island known in Jonathan Swift's day as "Serendip," as I was influenced by old movies and by a university teacher whom I admired, who was of Burgher descent. The Sri Lanka-born lecturer at University of Western Australia had studied in Britain and taught in Nigeria—before coming to Australia. I read of its flirtation with "radical" politics as well.

In short, I was primed for interest in a posting to Colombo, despite its limited importance to Australia. After my early retirement for medical reasons, I visited in 2011 (2012?) with a Chinese friend; it was my only visit. We stayed initially in the once-famous Galle Face Hotel in Colombo, before moving on to other towns. I saw the Australian High Commission, if only from the outside (it was a weekend).

After that, we drove south and east in a chartered taxi. The driver was a Sinhalese navy veteran of the civil war, a pleasant man. We went first to Galle, along the way seeing the lush scenery—but also the terrible damage left by the recent tsunami. There we stayed at an old guest-house that had been built in the 17th century for a Dutch merchant and his family. It offered Ayurvedic treatment, which I tried for my medical issues. (It offered great banana fritters, too.)

Then we went north and east to the equally old city of Kandy, an ancient capital, where a tooth of the Buddha is said to be preserved in a temple. Along the way, we passed the old tea-growing district, where we stopped for lunch. We stayed in an English-style "cottage" in the cooler hill-station climate. Although Kandy is best known for its (supposed) tooth of Buddha, I was drawn by its climate and its mists. We visited a lake that had been excavated by the British (according to a plaque there, that artificial lake had been created by an English engineer, rather like Isadore Kingdom Brunel). The nights there were cool enough to justify fireplaces.

From Kandy, we returned to Colombo, successfully avoiding near-accidents with reckless tuk-tuks. (Later I heard that our driver had been injured, in a tuk-tuk accident that he hadn't been able to avoid.) We drove straight to Bandaranaike International Airport, from where we returned to Perth via Singapore.

*July 2021; January 2023*

# Switzerland

I visited Switzerland in 1989 and 1990, having been invited by the World Economic Forum to organize a Western Australian delegation to the 1990 event. The first trip was to scout accommodation and check potential suppliers.

I stayed at a small hotel in Zurich for a few days, then travelled by train to Davos, where the meetings were held. Famously they are attended by the rich and famous: that year, people paid to hear Shirley MacLaine talk about astral travel, Senator Bill Bradley talk about US politics and basketball, and Akio Morita about Sony.

In 1990, I visited both places again, with the WA Premier of the day and members of the delegation he led. I met them at the airport and put them in buses and BMWs to go to Davos. There I met them again the next day, after escorting important cargo I had cleared through quarantine at Zurich Airport: wildflowers and pavlovas.

The 1990 event was well supported, due to Western Australia's growing reputation as a resources powerhouse. (But it didn't compete with Helmut Kohl.) Certainly the WA thing was fun to manage—although, for domestic reasons, the Premier returned to Perth to resign.

I learned the importance of patience from my time in Switzerland. Or, in the only Swiss-German phrase I remember: "Sprechen Sie Langshamme, Bitte" (Please speak more slowly).

*October 2021*

# Taiwan

I have visited Taiwan only once—in 1976—but I remember it well.

I flew alone from Hong Kong to Taipei. There I met up with "Tei-san," whom I had known at Keio University. We had talked of travelling together within Taiwan, but in the end I took a train alone from Taipei.

I went first to Taichung on the central coast. On the train was a family of well-fed Indians; I guessed the father was a diplomat. On arrival at Taichung, I asked directions of an older Chinese man in Japanese (after all, Taiwanese youths had been educated in Japanese until 30 years before).

From Taichung I took a tourist bus east to Taroko Gorge and Sun Moon Lake, well-known tourist destinations. They were spectacular and I much enjoyed seeing them.

On return to Taipei, with Tei-san and her father I visited Sun Yat-sen University, then the most prestigious college in Taiwan.

*August 2021*

*Michael and Nozomi at Swan River, Perth*

Part 7
# MICHAEL'S MUSINGS

# Coincidence

*The Makioka Sisters,* by Junichiro Tanizaki, is the great Japanese novel of the 20th Century. I've read it only in translation, but it is a masterful work. It's set in Osaka, centered on a once-wealthy family that is consumed by the task of marrying off a sister.

The context of the book—set in the 1930s—is the social change of the period, and the approaching war. As well as the Japanese family and their acquaintances, it features a German family who live nearby, until they're evacuated on the outbreak of war in the Pacific. One conjecture is that they were based on a real family the author had known (as is true in so many novels).

My old friend Kazuko told me a few years ago that she and her late husband had met that family after the war. They had been returning from a medical conference her husband had attended in Switzerland, when they fell into conversation on the train with a German woman and her child. It transpired that, as a teenager, the woman had been the model for the German family's daughter. It felt thrilling to be separated by only a couple of degrees from the plot of a great novel.

*December 2021*

# The Foolish Samaritan

I was living alone (for the first time in decades) when a person knocked on my door one afternoon in 2016. I wheeled to the door to see what the issue was. A young woman (at first, I thought she was a man, so deep was her voice) was there, and asked politely whether I had an old pair of pants she might borrow.

As an instinctive Samaritan, I said yes, hoping she was alright. I went inside, fetched an old pair of tracksuit-pants, and told her I didn't need them back. She seemed to want to explain and said she had wet her pants and couldn't walk back home because she had just been kicked out by her girlfriend.

At this point, I made my first real mistake. I asked whether the woman would like to use my shower. When she said that she would, I invited her in, albeit with a slowly sinking feeling. After she had showered and changed, I talked to her a little—after I had seen her walk past the second bedroom and carefully look at its contents. Then she said in an unguarded way that I should lock my electric scooter, as she had noticed, in the yard, that it was unlocked and would be very easy to steal.

By now I was fully alert and decided not to proceed with my earlier Good Samaritan intention, to invite her to return for a coffee (*duh!*). Later, on a brother's advice, I checked with the Fremantle Rangers and learned that she was an identified suspect...

*April 2021*

# Google, Etc. – Have the Robots Won?

I was startled recently when my mobile phone addressed me, out of the blue.

Unprovoked, it asked: "How can I help you?" (Clearly, it had been listening to my conversation with a friend.) Flippantly, I responded, "Oh, fuck off Google." Undeterred, the voice responded, "I'm sorry you feel that way."

A brief reflection says that one should never talk back to robots—that only encourages them (and discourages you). More serious thought leads to the conclusion that George Orwell was right—and well before 1984. But it's harder to know what to do against the Facebooks and Googles of this world.

Maybe governments should consider setting rules on privacy and consumer rights. But then, that might collide with vested interests...

*October 2021*

# *Issun Saki*

In 1990, I was preparing to take on management of the Western Australian offices in Japan. I had been working in Perth for an agency that more or less was responsible, and its boss hosted a farewell. On the day, I walked the short distance to the event with a female colleague who occupied a nearby office.

It had been clear for a while that Sue-Ellen was suffering from serious health problems, although still working. She was using a magnifying glass for reading and a stick to walk. She was said to have a scary-sounding illness called multiple sclerosis, that apparently afflicted an unlucky minority of people.

When we approached a pedestrian crossing, I offered Sue-Ellen my arm. She seemed glad to accept, although a couple of months before might have scorned it. At the reception, I remember that she offered some kind—and wise—words of encouragement. Quoting an old Irish expression, she said, "May the road rise up to meet you."

Sue-Ellen did not live for many more years. Looking back, I want to say from the Japanese, *"Issun saki"* meaning, "And the future is unknowable."

*February 22, 2019*

# Multiple Sclerosis Society

The MS Society in Western Australia—known by me as the FA Organization—is "successful" but failing. I call it that, because its slogan: "We Know Neuro" really should be changed. (I've said to a couple of its sensible staff that it should be: "We Know Fuck All.")

It is very successful at fund-raising and self-promotion, like many marketing organizations. But it has a poor record of selecting and training staff who ACTUALLY know the business of helping people with disease.

The former Chief Executive worked for a financial company and went into the "caring" sector from there. As a clever person, he trained others with good organizational and people skills, but who did NOT know neuro. His most notable achievement was to resign and get re-hired as irreplaceable, at a much higher salary.

Personally, I resigned from the MS Society twice this year in quick succession—in order to make my departure effective. I did that because it had good carers but very poor management. After discharge from hospital this year, I was left at home without help, despite a repeated promise that that would NOT happen.

*September 2021*

# My Decapitated Mule

On the windowsill in my bedroom is a small wooden mule that had no head until recently. It's an attractive Christian symbol, purchased more than fifty years ago in Jerusalem. It nicely balances a wooden Buddha, bought more recently in Sri Lanka.

The mule came from the only visit to Europe that we boys made with our parents, in 1967-8. We went on to Israel after seeing several parts of the continent but spent only three days in that country. The religious places we saw stayed in the mind too, but the day we spent in the Old City of Jerusalem for me was the most memorable day we spent in the country. I saw the animal in the store of an elderly Arab in East Jerusalem and bought it at a reasonable price, without any haggling. It is a charming thing that I took back to boarding school in Perth and have had ever since.

It wasn't to be found one day late last year, and a subsequent search led to a discovery of the animal under my bed. Unfortunately, the mule's head had been separated from its body, but happily it was made whole again by a friend and some wood glue. A small scar is the only reminder of the animal's trauma of last year. I hope to be forgiven in due course.

*March 2021*

# About the Author

*A Biographical Timeline*

- 1953 Born in Melbourne, Victoria

- 1955 Moved to Perth, Western Australia, and then to Hong Kong in 1958

- 1966-76 Educated at Scotch College, Perth, the University of WA, and Keio University, Tokyo

- 1979-86 With the Australian Department of Foreign Affairs, Canberra & Tokyo

- 1986-2001 With the WA Department of Resources Development, Perth & Tokyo

- 2001-2005 With North West Shelf LNG, Tokyo

- 2006-2008 With Inpex Corp., then retired with ill health.

# Tactile

This morning I woke rested.

That was fine, of course—

If not so common.


Sight & tactile scene were great;

They seemed Japan: subdued colours in

Garden & wall, lovely textures of

Sheet & flannel. Clear faces of people.


*By Michael John Walker*
*October 20, 2021*

Made in the USA
Las Vegas, NV
04 September 2024

94759108R10085